I0448465

December 2013

CRUISE VESSELS

Most Required Security and Safety Measures Have Been Implemented, but Concerns Remain About Crime Reporting

GAO-14-43

Highlights

Highlights of GAO-14-43, a report to congressional requesters

CRUISE VESSELS

Most Required Security and Safety Measures Have Been Implemented, but Concerns Remain About Crime Reporting

Why GAO Did This Study

In 2011, almost 11 million passengers took a cruise from a U.S. port. Media reports about passenger personal safety while aboard cruise vessels— including those related to the January 2012 grounding of the cruise vessel *Costa Concordia* off the coast of Italy, which resulted in 32 deaths— combined with the increasing number of passengers taking cruises has raised questions about passenger safety and security. With the enactment of the CVSSA in 2010, cruise vessels that visit U.S. ports were required to meet certain security and safety requirements, such as having rail heights of at least 42 inches and reporting allegations of certain crimes to the FBI. GAO was asked to review cruise vessel safety as well as security issues—related to keeping passengers safe from crime.

GAO reviewed (1) the extent to which the cruise vessel industry and federal agencies have implemented the CVSSA, and (2) any actions taken following the *Costa Concordia* accident to enhance the safety of cruise vessels visiting U.S. ports.

GAO reviewed the CVSSA and related agency and industry documents, and interviewed officials from the Coast Guard, FBI, CLIA, five cruise lines which accounted for over 80 percent of North American cruise vessel passengers in 2012, and two crime victim advocacy groups. The cruise lines were selected based on several factors including their volume of North American passengers. Crime victim advocacy groups were selected based on their knowledge about cruise ship crime issues. GAO is not making any recommendations in this report.

View GAO-14-43. For more information, contact Stephen L. Caldwell at (202) 512-9610 or caldwells@gao.gov.

What GAO Found

The cruise industry and federal agencies have implemented 11 of 15 Cruise Vessel Security and Safety Act (CVSSA) provisions, but implementation of 4 provisions requires the development of regulations and policy, and is underway. Officials from all five cruise lines GAO met with said most required measures were in place when the CVSSA was enacted. According to U.S. Coast Guard officials, a notice of proposed rulemaking is in development to address 3 of the 4 remaining provisions. The 3 provisions relate to technologies to (1) detect a person going overboard, (2) maintain a video surveillance system to assist in documenting crimes on the vessel, and (3) transmit communications and warnings from the ship to anyone in surrounding waters. A policy linked to the fourth provision on the certification of trainers who provide the CVSSA course on crime scene preservation to cruise line personnel, is, as of December 2013, undergoing review at the Department of Transportation. With respect to CVSSA crime-reporting requirements, the Federal Bureau of Investigation (FBI) and the Coast Guard have implemented these provisions as required. Accordingly, the agencies publish on a website information on reported crimes that are no longer under investigation. However, GAO identified some limitations in the usefulness of the publicly reported data. Specifically, (1) allegations for which investigations are not opened are never published; (2) the data are not timely—due to the length of the criminal justice process—and thus, crime data may be posted months or years after the alleged crime occurred and (3) the data reported are not put into context, such as a city's crime rate, to provide the public with the information needed to compare rates and make decisions. However, some cruise lines are making efforts to improve reported crime data. In August 2013, several cruise lines began voluntarily disclosing alleged crime data on their websites. Also, in July 2013, legislation was introduced to amend the CVSSA that would revise and expand crime-reporting requirements, among other items. As of November 2013, however, these actions were either new or pending. Thus, GAO could not assess whether, or to what extent, the voluntary reporting or potential legislation might provide more useful data than current requirements.

Following the *Costa Concordia* accident, the cruise industry, an international maritime organization, and the Coast Guard took actions to improve passenger safety. The Cruise Lines International Association (CLIA)—which represents over 98 percent of cruise lines in the United States—identified 10 safety-related policies in 2012 that were adopted by all member cruise lines by July 2013. These policies include improvements to vessel passage planning and life jacket stowage, among other things. The International Maritime Organization (IMO)—a United Nations agency responsible for maritime matters—has also adopted a regulation, effective January 2015, requiring passengers to participate in a safety and evacuation exercise (muster drill) prior to or immediately upon departure— rather than within 24 hours of departure. CLIA member cruise lines adopted a similar muster policy weeks after the *Costa Concordia* accident. The Coast Guard is monitoring IMO's consideration of additional regulations. The agency has also started witnessing predeparture muster drills and has reported no major concerns. In addition, the Coast Guard has worked with the cruise industry for several years to plan and hold disaster exercises, including one in April 2013 to practice a mass rescue from a cruise vessel.

_____ United States Government Accountability Office

Contents

Letter		1
	Background	6
	Cruise Industry and Federal Agencies Have Implemented Most CVSSA Provisions, and Additional Crime-Reporting Efforts Are Under Way	12
	The Cruise Industry Made Changes after the Costa Concordia Accident and Potential International Regulations Remain under Consideration	30
	Agency Comments	40
Appendix I	Key Stakeholders with Maritime Safety and Security Activities	42
Appendix II	Provisions in the Cruise Vessel Security and Safety Act	45
Appendix III	GAO Contact and Staff Acknowledgments	48

Tables

Table 1: Differing Viewpoints on the Cruise Vessel Security and Safety Act's (CVSSA) Man Overboard Technology Provision	15
Table 2: Differing Viewpoints on the Cruise Vessel Security and Safety Act's (CVSSA) Video Recording Requirements Provision	16
Table 3: Differing Viewpoints on the Cruise Vessel Security and Safety Act (CVSSA) Training Certification Provision	19
Table 4: Alleged CVSSA Crimes Reported to the FBI by Cruise Lines from January 2010 through September 2013	25
Table 5: Alleged CVSSA Crimes No Longer under Investigation by the FBI (Published on Coast Guard Website) from January 2010 through September 2013	25
Table 6: Stakeholders with Maritime Safety and Security Activities	42
Table 7: Summary of Provisions in the Cruise Vessel Security and Safety Act (CVSSA)	45

Figures

Figure 1: Regulatory Oversight Regime Affecting Cruise Vessels   7
Figure 2: Law Enforcement Process for Investigation of Cruise
          Crime within FBI's Jurisdiction   21
Figure 3: Timeline of CLIA Actions Relative to the Costa
          Concordia Accident   31
Figure 4: Timeline of IMO MSC Actions following the Costa
          Concordia Accident   37

Abbreviations

AAJ	American Association for Justice
BRM	Bridge Resource Management
CBP	Customs and Border Protection
CCTV	closed circuit television
CEO	chief executive officer
CLIA	Cruise Lines International Association
CVSSA	Cruise Vessel Security and Safety Act
FBI	Federal Bureau of Investigation
ICV	International Cruise Victim's Association
IMO	International Maritime Organization
ISM Code	International Safety Management Code
MARAD	Maritime Administration
MSC	Maritime Safety Committee
NPRM	Notice of Proposed Rulemaking
NTSB	National Transportation Safety Board
OMB	Office of Management and Budget
RFI	Request for Information
SMS	safety management system
SOLAS	International Convention for the Safety of Life at Sea
STD	sexually transmitted disease
UCR	Uniform Crime Reports

GAO U.S. GOVERNMENT ACCOUNTABILITY OFFICE

441 G St. N.W.
Washington, DC 20548

December 20, 2013

The Honorable John D. Rockefeller IV
Chairman
The Honorable John Thune
Ranking Member
Committee on Science, Commerce and Transportation
United States Senate

The Honorable Bennie Thompson
Ranking Member
Committee on Homeland Security
House of Representatives

The Honorable Doris O. Matsui
House of Representatives

The popularity of cruise vessels as a vacation option continues to grow. Since 1980, the cruise industry has had an average annual passenger growth rate of 7.6 percent, and in 2011, over 16 million passengers traveled aboard cruise vessels worldwide.[1] About 10.9 million of these passengers traveled from U.S. ports.[2] Media reports about passenger personal safety while aboard cruise vessels, combined with the increasing number of cruise vessel passengers and the January 2012 *Costa Concordia* cruise vessel grounding off the coast of Italy, which claimed 32 lives, raised questions about personal security and passenger safety when aboard cruise vessels. According to the Federal Bureau of Investigation (FBI), from 2005 through 2010, sexual assaults and physical assaults on cruise vessels were the leading cruise vessel crimes investigated and reported by the FBI. However, the public was often not aware of these crimes because the federal government did not require information about them to be published. Moreover, cruise vessels

---

[1]Cruise Lines International Association (CLIA), *2011 CLIA Cruise Market Overview* (Fort Lauderdale, Florida: 2011). Passenger numbers for various years can be found on CLIA's website at http://www.cruising.org/regulatory/industry-welcome.

[2]U.S. Department of Transportation Maritime Administration, *North American Cruise Statistical Snapshot, 2011*(Washington, D.C: March 2012) Data on the number of cruise passengers for 2012 were not available because the Department of Transportation's Maritime Administration no longer collects this information.

carrying U.S. passengers often travel to foreign ports before returning to the United States, a fact that can introduce the possible involvement of law enforcement from a variety of foreign countries—in addition to the federal and local law enforcement agencies that may be involved if a crime occurs during a voyage. The involvement or potential involvement of foreign governments can add to the confusion of crime victims as they attempt to navigate various justice systems.

The Cruise Vessel Security and Safety Act (CVSSA), enacted in July 2010, requires cruise lines operating ships that visit U.S. ports and the federal government to take certain actions related to these issues.[3] For example, the CVSSA requires the cruise lines to report allegations of certain crimes to the FBI and the United States Coast Guard as well as to ensure that passengers have key information available to them—such as U.S. embassy contact information for all of the countries on the cruise vessel itinerary—and to implement specific personal security measures onboard such as ensuring that all stateroom doors have peepholes, among other things.[4] The CVSSA also requires that the Coast Guard maintain a website that provides a numerical accounting of certain crimes that have been reported by cruise lines, but are no longer under FBI investigation.[5] The CVSSA places much of the responsibility for implementing the law with the Coast Guard and FBI. The Coast Guard is the federal agency responsible for a wide array of maritime safety and security activities, including those involving cruise vessels and their landside facilities, while the FBI is responsible for investigating certain cruise vessel crimes, among other responsibilities.

In addition to the issue of personal security of passengers, the January 2012 grounding of the cruise vessel *Costa Concordia* off the coast of Italy

---

[3]Pub. L. No. 111-207, 124 Stat. 2243. The CVSSA applies to cruise vessels that are authorized to carry at least 250 passengers, have onboard sleeping facilities for each passenger, are on a voyage that embarks or disembarks passengers in the United States, and are not engaged on a coastwise voyage. 46 U.S.C. § 3507(k)(1). Security, as it relates to the CVSSA and this report, is concerned with personal security from crime rather than threats of terrorism. We have previously reported on the issue of cruise vessel security as it relates to threats of terrorism. See GAO, *Maritime Security: Varied Actions Taken to Enhance Cruise Ship Security, but Some Concerns Remain*, GAO-10-400 (Washington, D.C.: Apr. 9, 2010).

[4]46 U.S.C. §§ 3507(g)(3)(A), 3507(c)(2), 3507(a)(1)(B).

[5]Id. at § 3507(g)(4).

raised questions about vessel management and the procedures for safeguarding passengers in emergency situations. For example, although international maritime law requires all passengers to be evacuated within 30 minutes of an order to abandon a vessel, the Italian government reported that the evacuation of the *Costa Concordia* took over 6 hours. The accident resulted in the death of 32 passengers. The Italian government investigated the accident and reported in May 2013 on numerous lapses in emergency procedures and management, including problems with vessel evacuation, voyage planning, and emergency communication.

You requested that we review the implementation of the CVSSA as well as any safety actions taken by federal government agencies and the cruise industry following the *Costa Concordia* accident. This report examines the following questions:

- To what extent have the cruise industry and federal agencies taken actions to implement the requirements of the CVSSA?

- What actions, if any, have federal agencies and the cruise industry taken to enhance the safety of cruise vessels visiting U.S. ports as a result of the *Costa Concordia* accident?

To address both objectives, we conducted visits to four cruise vessel ports, which we selected in large part because of their high cruise traffic and passenger embarkation volume, among other things—Los Angeles, California; Miami, Florida; Fort Lauderdale, Florida; and Seattle, Washington. To understand how the Coast Guard checks for CVSSA compliance and other safety issues on cruise vessels, we accompanied Coast Guard officials on cruise vessel exams in the Port of Los Angeles and Port Everglades, the port for Fort Lauderdale. During these visits, we interviewed security and safety officials from five cruise lines to understand how they implemented the provisions of the CVSSA and what safety changes they have implemented as a result of the *Costa Concordia* accident.[6] Additionally, we interviewed Coast Guard officials in

---

[6]Throughout the report we refer to these companies as cruise lines. However, they include two cruise corporations that are parent companies to several cruise lines or brands. Additionally, we conducted an interview with a subsidiary company of one corporation related to CVSSA implementation and security, but for purposes of this report, we have categorized this interview under the corporation. The five cruise lines we interviewed represent over 80 percent of North American cruise vessel passengers in 2012.

the field and in headquarters on their role in implementing the CVSSA, any challenges encountered during implementation, and any actions taken following the *Costa Concordia* accident. We also interviewed officials from the Cruise Lines International Association (CLIA)—which currently represents over 98 percent of the cruise industry operating in the United States—for their perspective on the impact of the CVSSA and to discuss the safety changes they have implemented among their members as a result of the *Costa Concordia* accident. Finally, during our visits to cruise vessel ports, we also interviewed FBI and local law enforcement agency officials to discuss their role in handling crime aboard cruise vessels. The information we obtained from personnel at the ports and the cruise lines cannot be generalized across all U.S. ports and the cruise industry—although CLIA does represent a substantial portion of the industry—but the information provided us with a perspective on the implementation of the CVSSA as well as any changes resulting from the *Costa Concordia* accident.

To address the first objective, we reviewed relevant documents, guidance, and policy from federal agencies, such as the Coast Guard's policy letter on CVSSA implementation procedures. Additionally, we reviewed the provisions in the CVSSA and assessed the extent to which federal agencies and cruise lines were implementing those provisions. We also analyzed alleged and published cruise vessel crime data obtained from the FBI. Specifically, we analyzed all CVSSA crimes reported to the FBI from January 2008 through September 2013 (pre- and post-CVSSA implementation) as well as analyzed for the same time period the number of closed cases that appeared on the Coast Guard's public website. To determine the reliability of these data, we interviewed FBI and cruise line officials familiar with the data regarding their procedures for obtaining, analyzing, and reporting cruise vessel crime data. We determined that the data were sufficiently reliable for our purposes.[7] While the publication of the CVSSA crime data is consistent with the law, these data have some limitations. These limitations were identified through our independent analysis, as well as through comments from officials at the FBI, CLIA, the cruise lines we met with, and a crime victim advocacy groups. We discuss these limitations later in this report.

---

[7]The data posted on the Coast Guard website were provided to the Coast Guard from the FBI and were a subset ("cases no longer under investigation") of the information provided to us for analysis. The Coast Guard reported that it had no role in verifying the accuracy of the information.

We interviewed Coast Guard officials as well as representatives of two victim advocacy groups and two academic researchers who have written extensively on cruise vessel crime for their perspectives on the implementation of the CVSSA. The interest groups and researchers were selected based on their knowledge about cruise vessel crime—either advocating for victims or researching cruise crime trends.[8] We also interviewed officials from the the Department of Transportation's Maritime Administration (MARAD)—which works to improve and strengthen the U.S. marine transportation system—to determine its role in implementing the CVSSA and discuss any challenges MARAD had encountered.

To address the second objective, we reviewed relevant documents and policies from CLIA and the selected cruise lines, including the safety measures that CLIA introduced after the *Costa Concordia* accident. We also reviewed documents from the International Maritime Organization (IMO)—a United Nations agency that specializes in maritime issues—as well as the *Costa Concordia* marine casualty investigation report issued by the Italian government in 2013. We interviewed Department of State and National Transportation Safety Board (NTSB) officials to understand their agencies' roles in relation to cruise vessel safety and the *Costa Concordia* accident. During our port visits, we also interviewed officials from two classification societies to better understand their roles in ensuring cruise vessel safety.[9] We also witnessed a cruise vessel mass rescue exercise, conducted by the Coast Guard, which involved numerous cruise line personnel, federal agency personnel, and local authorities in the Bahamas. The exercise was part of a series of mass rescue operation–based exercises designed to educate and prepare

[8]While the information we obtained from these groups and individuals cannot be generalized across the entire cruise industry, it provided us with varying perspectives on issues associated with cruise vessel crime and CVSSA implementation.

[9]A classification society verifies the structural strength and integrity of essential parts of a vessel's hull and appendages, and the reliability and function of the propulsion and steering systems, power generation, and those other features and auxiliary systems that have been built into the vessel in order to maintain essential services onboard. Classification societies do this through the development and application of their own rules and by verifying compliance with international and national statutory regulations. We interviewed two classification societies that were headquartered in the Miami area—the location of one of our visits. While the information we obtained from the classification societies cannot be generalized across the entire cruise industry, it did provide us with a perspective on issues associated with cruise vessel safety.

participants for a potential catastrophic event—similar to the *Costa Concordia* accident—involving a mass rescue operation at sea.

We conducted this performance audit from January 2013 to December 2013 in accordance with generally accepted government auditing standards. Those standards require that we plan and perform the audit to obtain sufficient, appropriate evidence to provide a reasonable basis for our findings and conclusions based on our audit objectives. We believe that the evidence obtained provides a reasonable basis for our findings and conclusions based on our audit objectives.

Background

Many Stakeholders Involved in Cruise Vessel Safety and Security Regulation

International, national, state, and local requirements regulate maritime safety and security. At the international level, IMO is responsible for developing an international maritime regulatory framework. IMO member states (nations) have adopted the International Convention for the Safety of Life at Sea (SOLAS), which is designed to help ensure maritime security and safety worldwide. Among other things, SOLAS provides that companies and vessels should comply with the requirements of the International Safety Management Code (ISM Code), which was adopted by IMO in 1993. Federal laws, regulations, and guidance direct federal agencies and vessel operators within U.S. ports and waters, and state and local requirements may also further direct activities of vessel operators within their jurisdictions.

The enforcement of safety and security requirements for all maritime vessels is governed by two different systems: flag state control and port state control. A flag state that signed on to the SOLAS Convention has responsibility for verifying that vessels flying its flag meet international safety and security standards and that the flag state's standards are at least as stringent as those included in the convention's ISM Code. A port state is the country where a port is located. Port state control is the process by which a nation exercises its authority over foreign-flagged vessels operating in waters subject to the port state's jurisdiction. Port state control is generally intended to ensure that these visiting vessels comply with the various international and domestic requirements established to help ensure the safety of the visited port, its environment, and its personnel. Figure 1 shows the regulatory oversight regime affecting cruise vessels; however, there are many additional international and domestic stakeholders with roles contributing to the security and safety of cruise vessels. For a list of key stakeholders and their activities, see appendix I.

Figure 1: Regulatory Oversight Regime Affecting Cruise Vessels

Regulatory structure

International Maritime Organization (IMO)

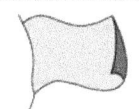

IMO is the United Nations specialized agency with responsibility for the safety and security of shipping and the prevention of marine pollution by vessels. IMO is responsible for creating international regulations for maritime safety.

Flag state

A cruise vessel must be registered to a country. However, the country of registration is at the discretion of the owner of the vessel. Once a country, or flag state, is chosen, the vessel is bound to that country's jurisdiction and control in administrative and technical matters over vessels flying its flag.

Classification society

Classification societies are private, third-party organizations whose main function is to inspect the vessel at regular intervals to ensure its seaworthiness. They verify that the vessel's structure and machinery are being maintained as required by classification societies' rules. Classification societies may, if authorized by the vessel's flag state, also conduct safety audits for compliance with international regulations.

Owner

The vessel owner has the overall responsibility for the safety and integrity of a vessel, including the manner in which it is operated and maintained. As required by the International Safety Management Code, the vessel owner is to carry out annual internal safety audits.

U.S. Coast Guard port state control

The Coast Guard conducts preconstruction concept review, midconstruction inspections, and an initial operating inspection for foreign-flagged vessels that plan to visit U.S. ports. Once the cruise vessel is in service, Coast Guard inspectors board the vessel (at least annually) to check that the vessel's major systems are in compliance with applicable international standards and domestic requirements, and that the crew possesses sufficient proficiency to safely operate the vessel.

Source: GAO analysis of regulatory entities affecting cruise vessels; Art Explosion (clip art)

The Coast Guard administers the U.S. port state control program for foreign-flagged cruise vessels that enter U.S. waters or a U.S. port, to enforce maritime safety and security in the United States.[10] The Coast Guard exercises this enforcement through port state control activities, which include initial, annual, and periodic examinations of foreign flag cruise vessels. These exams allow the Coast Guard to examine vessels at various times:

- **Initial exams:** Conducted on vessels with potential U.S. itineraries, these exams include concept reviews during the very earliest stages of design, preconstruction plan reviews by Coast Guard naval architects and fire protection engineers, and mid-construction inspections at the shipbuilder's yard by Coast Guard marine inspectors.

- **Annual inspection:** The Coast Guard inspects each cruise vessel visiting the United States at least twice a year. The first inspection, an annual inspection, focuses on the vessel's fire protection, lifesaving, and emergency systems as well as any modifications to the vessel that would affect its structural fire protection and means of escape.

- **Periodic inspection:** The second Coast Guard inspection, a periodic inspection, focuses on the performance of the officers and crew, with specific attention paid to their training and knowledge of the vessel's emergency procedures, fire fighting, lifesaving systems, and performance during drills.

From January 2008 through March 2013, the Coast Guard performed 1,208 cruise vessel examinations (71 initial, 673 annual, and 464 periodic) and identified 1,802 deficiencies. Nearly half of these deficiencies were related to fire-fighting systems. For example, according to the Coast Guard's Cruise Ship National Center of Expertise, the most common deficiency identified in 2012 was the improper operation of fire screen doors. In 2011, the most commonly identified deficiency was the improper stowage of combustibles. According to Coast Guard officials, most deficiencies are corrected on the spot or within the time frames allowed by the Coast Guard. Moreover, officials reported that the Coast Guard rarely detains cruise vessels based on substandard compliance— for example, from January 2008 through March 2013, they have detained

---

[10]Almost all cruise vessels operating in and out of U.S. ports are foreign flagged.

seven cruise vessels as a result of their 1,208 cruise vessel examinations. Four of the seven cruise vessels made corrections and were released from detention the same day, while the others took 2, 3, and 8 days to make corrections.[11]

As part of its regulatory role, the Coast Guard also maintains data on marine casualties (accidents) that occur upon the navigable waters of the United States and its territories or possessions, or whenever an accident involves a U.S. vessel. Coast Guard regulations require that certain types of accidents be reported to the Coast Guard—including accidents that result in the loss of main propulsion or primary steering, or that materially and adversely affect the vessel's seaworthiness, among other things.[12] Our analysis of Coast Guard data shows that from January 2008 through March 2013, there were 256 marine casualties that involved cruise vessels: 128 of these were classified as failures of equipment or material; 64 were classified as accidents that caused damage to the environment (mostly discharge of oil); and 64 were classified in a variety of other categories—such as fire, loss of electrical power, or collision.[13]

Cruise Vessel Security and Safety Act Added to Regulatory Framework

Enacted in July 2010, the CVSSA, as discussed above, required cruise lines and federal agencies to take certain actions designed to further bolster the security and safety of U.S. passengers aboard cruise vessels. The CVSSA applies to all passenger vessels that are authorized to carry at least 250 passengers, have onboard sleeping facilities for each

---

[11]According to Coast Guard officials, analysis shows that foreign cruise vessels have roughly 70 percent fewer deficiencies than other types of foreign-flagged vessels, and are less likely to be detained. Additionally, given the quick turnaround that can occur with cruise vessels at ports and the amount of time needed to conduct an inspection, Coast Guard inspections are scheduled in advance.

[12] 46 C.F.R. pt. 4.

[13]This analysis excludes 786 marine casualties that were classified as "personnel casualties," where one or more individuals were injured or died as the result of existing medical conditions or contact with the vessel as a result of a fall, among other things. Although in some instances personnel casualty data may be related to CVSSA crimes— such as when injury or death is the result of a CVSSA crime—we did not include a comparison of marine casualty data to CVSSA crime data for two reasons. First, there is overlap but not a direct correlation between some of the data associated with personnel casualties and the required crime-reporting categories in the CVSSA. Second, there are differences in reporting requirements for marine casualties versus CVSSA crime, based on the ownership and registry of the vessel, the nationality of the person(s) involved, and the location of the vessel at the time of the incident.

passenger, are on voyages that embark or disembark passengers from the United States, and are not engaged on coastwise voyages.[14] The CVSSA includes 15 provisions aimed at, among other things, increasing information available to passengers—such as requiring cruise lines to provide contact information in passenger staterooms for local embassies and providing crime victims with free and immediate access to sexual assault hotlines—as well as provisions requiring training to increase the capability of a cruise vessel's crew to document crimes and preserve crime scenes. Many CVSSA requirements are aimed at the cruise lines and were effective with CVSSA enactment or by January 27, 2012—18 months after CVSSA's enactment. The topics addressed by these 15 provisions are listed below (for a more detailed summary of these provisions please see app. II):

- Rail heights
- Peepholes
- Security latches and time-sensitive keys
- Capture of images/detection of passengers who have fallen overboard
- Acoustical hailing and warning devices
- Video recording requirements
- Availability of passenger safety information
- Medical treatment for victims of sexual assault
- Access to information and communications for victims of sexual assault
- Confidentiality of sexual assault examination and support information
- Logbook details and requirement to report alleged crimes
- Crew access to passenger staterooms
- Crime data on Coast Guard website and link on cruise line websites
- MARAD certification of crew training on crime scene preservation
- Crew training on crime scene preservation

---

[14]46 U.S.C. § 3507(k)(1). A coastwise voyage is defined as a voyage in which a vessel in the usual course of her employment proceeds from one port or place in the United States to another port or place in the United States or from a port or place in a possession to another port or place in the same possession, and passes outside the line dividing inland waters from the high seas (a voyage exclusively on the Great Lakes excepted), as well as a voyage in which a vessel proceeds from a port or place in the United States or its possessions and passes outside the line dividing inland waters from the high seas and navigates on the high seas, and then returns to the same port or place.

Costa Concordia Accident Identified Numerous Potential Safety Shortcomings

On January 13, 2012, an Italian-flagged cruise vessel, the *Costa Concordia*, ran aground with over 4,000 passengers and crew onboard off the coast of Giglio Island, Italy. The vessel was so badly damaged that five contiguous watertight compartments—which housed machinery and equipment vital for the propulsion and steering of the vessel—rapidly flooded. The vessel then lost propulsion and suffered intermittent power outages, as the emergency backup systems could not handle an emergency on such a scale. The accident resulted in 32 deaths, including 2 U.S. citizens.

The *Costa Concordia* accident triggered an investigation led by the Italian government to ascertain the reasons that the vessel went aground. In May 2013, the Italian government issued its findings and recommendations. The investigation found that the root cause of the accident rested with the vessel's master for transiting too close to the coastline. According to the investigation, the accident was compounded because of poor emergency management by the master, some staff deck officers, and the vessel's hotel director. However, the report also offered additional recommendations, including improvements in bridge resource management, emergency power generation, and search and rescue operations, among other things.[15]

---

[15]A vessel's bridge is the part of the vessel from which it is steered and navigated. Bridge Resource Management (BRM) is the effective management and utilization of all resources, human and technical, available to the bridge team (those employed on the bridge) to ensure the safe completion of the vessel's voyage. BRM focuses on bridge officers' skills such as teamwork, team building, communication, leadership, decision making, and resource management and incorporates these into the larger picture of organizational and regulatory management.

Cruise Industry and Federal Agencies Have Implemented Most CVSSA Provisions, and Additional Crime-Reporting Efforts Are Under Way

In 2011, the Coast Guard issued guidance on most of the provisions in the CVSSA, and the cruise lines had already implemented most of the safety measures required by the law. However, as of December 2013, the Coast Guard and MARAD were in the process of developing and publicizing new regulations before moving forward with the implementation of the remaining provisions related to items such as new technology and training certifications required or authorized by the CVSSA. Provisions regarding the publication of information on crimes on cruise vessels have been fully implemented by the FBI and Coast Guard in accordance with the law. Even so, efforts are under way that could address remaining concerns related to the thoroughness, timeliness, and context of reported crime data.

The Coast Guard Issued CVSSA Guidance, and Cruise Lines Have Implemented Most CVSSA Requirements

The Coast Guard issued guidance for 11 of the 15 CVSSA provisions in June 2011.[16] The Coast Guard guidance was issued in the form of internal Coast Guard policy letters with the main purpose of providing instructions to Coast Guard port state control officers regarding CVSSA requirements.[17] Guidance was provided in the following 11 areas: (1) rail heights; (2) peepholes in passenger stateroom doors, (3) security latches and time-sensitive keys for stateroom doors, (4) safety information provided to passengers, (5) medical licensing and proper equipment to perform sexual assault exams, (6) patient access to information and communications in the event of sexual assault, (7) confidentiality of sexual assault examination and support information, (8) crew access to passenger staterooms, (9) logbook and reporting requirements for CVSSA crimes, (10) availability of crime data on the Coast Guard's website and the link on cruise lines' webpages to the Coast Guard's

---

[16]CVSSA required Coast Guard to issue guidelines, training curricula, and inspection and certification procedures necessary to carry out the requirements of the law. 46 U.S.C. § 3507(i). Pursuant to the guidance, two of the provisions (rail heights and peepholes or other means of identification on stateroom doors) were not to be enforced by Coast Guard inspectors during their exams until January 2012; the remaining provisions were to be enforced from the date of enactment of the CVSSA, in July 2010 (although implementation guidelines from the Coast Guard did not come out until June 2011). The requirement for security latches/time-sensitive keys on stateroom doors applies only to those vessels where the keel was laid on or after July 27, 2010.

[17]The Coast Guard posted the policy guidance on its external website, so it was publicly available to cruise lines and others as well.

website,[18] and (11) training standards and curricula—which resulted in the development of the required course on crime scene preservation.[19] Coast Guard officials stated that the guidance was necessary to help clarify some aspects of the CVSSA, especially in those areas that are outside the Coast Guard's normal area of expertise. For example, the guidance provides specific questions for inspectors to ask medical personnel to verify that adequate training, equipment, and medicine are in place in the event of a sexual assault.

Officials from all five of the cruise lines we spoke with, as well as CLIA, told us that there were minor issues with implementing these 11 CVSSA requirements and that most of the safety and security measures required by the law were already in place when the CVSSA was enacted, in July 2010. For example, each of the cruise line officials we met with told us that their vessels already were in compliance with most CVSSA provisions including having peepholes in stateroom doors, using certified medical personnel for sexual assault exams, and carrying rape kits onboard. As a result, according to all of the cruise lines we spoke with, meeting the CVSSA deadline for most of the requirements was not difficult. In the case where a modification was needed to meet a CVSSA requirement, the cruise lines we spoke with described the modification as minor. For example, officials from CLIA stated that, for the most part, the rail heights on their members' vessels already met the 42-inch height specified in the CVSSA. In one case, officials from a cruise line identified isolated locations where the rail height was below the requirement—such as around entrance gangways and by lifeboat stations—and thus they took steps to modify the railing height to meet the new standard. CLIA officials also reported that developing security information guides for passenger staterooms required a moderate amount of effort for the cruise lines because of the variations in their vessels' itineraries, which required cruise lines to collect and update information for all of their vessels' ports

---

[18]Policy guidance was not issued in this area; however, Coast Guard officials told us they maintain a website with the FBI's cruise vessel crime data and that they did an initial check of all cruise lines' webpages to ensure they had a link to this Coast Guard crime data website.

[19]Three federal agencies were involved in creating the required course on crime scene preservation: the Coast Guard, the FBI, and MARAD. The Coast Guard coordinated the development of the course, the FBI provided much of the content for the course, and MARAD contributed its expertise in writing and structuring training courses, according to Coast Guard officials.

of call. Additionally, officials from one cruise line we spoke with discussed going beyond what the CVSSA requires. For example, this cruise line told us it was involved in discussions with officials from a victim advocacy group to evaluate and enhance the cruise line's procedures for preventing sexual assault and responding to sexual assault allegations. Additionally, this cruise line also told us it uses strict criteria to credential its professional staff to meet at least the minimum guidelines of the American College of Emergency Physicians and uses outside vendor software to help ensure credentials are kept up to date. Furthermore, these officials stated that an electronic medical record system is being introduced to improve the documentation and accessibility of health care information for guests and crew.

The Coast Guard and MARAD Are in the Process of Developing Regulations and Policy for Four CVSSA Provisions

There are four CVSSA provisions that require the development of regulations and policy for enforcement, and these are in development by the Coast Guard and MARAD. These provisions are (1) man overboard technology, which detects and alerts the crew to a person falling overboard; (2) video recording requirements, which are to assist in documenting crimes on the vessel and in providing evidence for the prosecution of such crimes; (3) acoustical hailing and warning devices, which provide communication capability around a vessel operating in high-risk waters; and (4) certification of training providers that teach the CVSSA training course on crime prevention, detection, evidence preservation, and reporting.[20] The Coast Guard is responsible for developing regulations for the first three provisions, while MARAD is responsible for developing policy for the training certification provision.

Coast Guard CVSSA Provisions

The Coast Guard issued a Request for Information (RFI) in May 2011 to obtain the public's input on the CVSSA requirements on man overboard technology and video recording because they involved complex technology and the CVSSA language was not specific enough, according to Coast Guard officials, for them to use it to verify compliance on cruise vessels. In response to its RFI, the Coast Guard received comments from nine entities: CLIA, two cruise victim advocacy groups, five companies stating that they had effective technology in these areas, and one private citizen. In addition to the RFI responses, officials that we interviewed from

---

[20]High-risk waters are defined by the Coast Guard as waters with a high risk of terrorism, piracy, or armed robbery against vessels.

CLIA, cruise lines, and cruise victim advocacy groups also provided insights on some of the challenges associated with two of the technology provisions of the CVSSA. Comments from the RFI as well as additional information provided to us from interested stakeholders are discussed in tables 1 and 2:

Table 1: Differing Viewpoints on the Cruise Vessel Security and Safety Act's (CVSSA) Man Overboard Technology Provision

Man overboard technology

CVSSA language: The vessel shall integrate technology that can be used for capturing images of passengers or detecting passengers who have fallen overboard, to the extent that such technology is available.[a]

Cruise Lines International Association's (CLIA) request for information (RFI) comments	CLIA noted that there are two different parts to the man overboard technology: image capturing and detection. CLIA stated that the technology exists to reliably capture images of people falling overboard through closed circuit television (CCTV), thermal imaging, and so forth. However, the technology to reliably detect persons as they are in the process of going overboard does not presently exist. CLIA believes the technology is not yet reliable in a maritime environment because of the movement of a vessel, weather and sun glare, and lens encrustation caused by saltwater, among other things.
Cruise victim advocacy group's RFI comments	An official from the International Cruise Victim's Association (ICV) stated that all CCTV systems of public areas should be monitored at all times and recorded by qualified shipboard security personnel in a dedicated watch center. Such a system would provide a safety blanket that envelops the vessel, making it impossible for someone to go overboard without being seen on a video camera.
Five cruise lines interviewed comments	All five of the cruise lines we met with agreed with CLIA's perspective that the technology to detect persons as they are in the process of going overboard is not yet reliable. However, officials from four of the five cruise lines we met with have or are currently testing different technologies onboard their cruise vessels. Officials from four of the five cruise lines also said one problem with the technology relates to the potential impact of false readings, both positive and negative. Specifically, one cruise line official commented that if cruise lines are going to be required to invest significant amounts of money in man overboard technology they want to be sure it does not produce inaccurate results that could result in increased operational costs such as conducting unnecessary searches or disrupting an itinerary, among other costs. Similarly, if the technology failed to detect a passenger who had gone overboard, and as a result the vessel failed to conduct a search for that person, this type of error could expose the cruise line to costly litigation.

Source: RFI comments provided to Coast Guard and GAO interviews.

[a]46 U.S.C. § 3507(a)(1)(D).

Table 2: Differing Viewpoints on the Cruise Vessel Security and Safety Act's (CVSSA) Video Recording Requirements Provision

Video recording requirements
CVSSA language: Requirement to maintain surveillance.—The owner of a vessel to which this section applies shall maintain a video surveillance system to assist in documenting crimes on the vessel and in providing evidence for the prosecution of such crimes, as determined by the Secretary.[a]

Cruise Lines International Association's (CLIA) request for information (RFI) comments	CLIA said that two main factors must be considered in developing regulations for a video surveillance system: locations on the vessel that should be under video surveillance and the length of time that images should be retained. CLIA commented that each vessel is different in size, layout, and design as well as the number and demographics of its passengers, and the type and location of prior crime allegations. As a result, CLIA commented that there should be a risk-based approach, rather than arbitrary standards, that guide video recording requirements. CLIA also recommended a video retention period of 7 days, as the average cruise length of its member lines is 7.2 days.
Cruise victim advocacy groups' RFI comments	Cruise victim advocacy groups state they would like to see more video cameras onboard, and the cameras monitored continuously. Two advocacy groups that provided RFI comments on the video recording requirements differed about how long video recordings should be kept. One group stated that the video recordings should be retained for 30 days; another stated the recordings should be retained for 90 days.
Five cruise lines interviewed comments	Officials from two cruise lines we spoke with said that most crimes are reported within 1 to 2 weeks after they occur, so video retention requirements longer than that would be unnecessary. Specifically, officials from one cruise line we spoke with commented that its current retention storage is 14 days, but if it was to double the retention period to 28 days, it would be at a one-time cost of $21.7 million. This cruise line also noted that it is standard practice to keep video footage indefinitely if it is tied to an ongoing investigation. This cruise line also reported that ensuring that video footage of a crime is maintained is generally not an issue, as 95 percent of crimes are reported to it within 24 hours. Officials from two cruise lines also said that because of the large number of cameras onboard it is not feasible to have continuous monitoring.

Source: RFI comments provided to Coast Guard and GAO interviews.

[a]46 U.S.C. § 3507(b).

The Coast Guard's RFI did not solicit feedback on the final provision, on acoustical hailing; however, Coast Guard officials told us that this provision would still be part of the final regulation as the technology already exists for acoustical hailing and warning devices. The term "high-risk waters" used in the provision was problematic to some cruise victim advocacy groups, according to Coast Guard officials, as they perceived the definition to be different from the Coast Guard's definition. For example, Coast Guard officials said that some cruise victim advocacy groups believe that those places that may be high-risk terrorism targets near land should be considered high-risk waters (e.g., New York Harbor and waterways). However, Coast Guard officials told us they have a long-standing definition of high-risk waters, and that they are typically waters where terrorism, piracy, and armed robbery occur (i.e., the waters off the Horn of Africa, etc.). Therefore, Coast Guard officials said that they felt it was necessary to include this provision in the proposed rule to allow for public comments because it was not clear from the law how the provision should be implemented.

In July 2013, Coast Guard officials told us that they had drafted a Notice of Proposed Rulemaking (NPRM) that will encompass these three provisions of the CVSSA. They added that the regulation will likely be performance based—focusing on what must be achieved—rather than prescriptive. Coast Guard officials noted that the NPRM is currently going through final agency review. According to the website of the Office of Management and Budget (OMB), which is the final reviewer in the rulemaking process, the NPRM will be issued in June 2014. There is no timetable for when the final regulation will be issued.

All cruise line officials we spoke with reported that one of their key frustrations with the implementation of the CVSSA was not having timely information related to these three technology areas of the CVSSA. They expressed concern with how long it has taken to develop the regulations as well as concern about the lack of interim communication from the Coast Guard on the status of the rulemaking process. Cruise line officials stated that this affects their business, and that they want to be in full compliance with the law. Coast Guard officials commented that the time they have taken to develop the proposed rule was to ensure that they were adequately addressing CVSSA requirements and incorporating all viewpoints, while MARAD officials said that the time they took was to determine the best approach for implementation. Furthermore, Coast Guard officials told us that once a rulemaking process is under way, federal agencies generally do not discuss it with outside parties to avoid concerns regarding ex parte communications. According to Coast Guard officials, engaging with outside parties to update them on the process, as cruise line officials wished had been done, could hinder transparency, unless the agency gave all parties and the public the same opportunity to comment and provide information.

While the Coast Guard is drafting its NPRM to address these three outstanding CVSSA provisions, in July 2013, legislation was introduced that would amend the video recording requirements of the CVSSA, among other items.[21] The proposed bills detail requirements for placement of video surveillance equipment on cruise vessels, access to

---

[21]S.1340, 113th Cong. (2013); H.R. 2800, 113th Cong. (2013).

video records, and video retention standards, among other items. As of December 2013, the two bills have been referred to the Senate Committee on Commerce, Science and Transportation and the House Committee on Transportation and Infrastructure's Subcommittee on Coast Guard and Maritime Transportation, respectively, and have not been voted on. It is unclear what effect these bills may have on the impending regulation from the Coast Guard if they become law.

MARAD CVSSA Provision

For the fourth CVSSA provision, MARAD issued a notice of proposed new policy in the *Federal Register* in May 2013 for certifying providers of the CVSSA training course on crime prevention, detection, evidence preservation, and reporting.[22] While the CVSSA did not mandate that MARAD develop a training provider certification—the language of the CVSSA states that MARAD "may" develop a certification—MARAD officials stated that they were intent on pursuing certification because there were requests from both the Coast Guard and CLIA to provide clarity on the certification portion of the CVSSA. MARAD proposed a voluntary certification program for training providers to assure the general public that passenger cruise vessel security and safety personnel have received training that is in strict compliance with the CVSSA-mandated model training course. According to MARAD, certification would serve to assist the cruise industry in identifying and obtaining qualified training services. Training providers seeking to be certified by MARAD would be required to submit training plans and supporting information for review. If the training provider's plans meet the CVSSA model course criteria, the agency would offer its certification subject to the training provider entering into an agreement that, in addition to other terms, would subject the organization to program audits. Four comments were received on the proposed policy from CLIA, ICV, the American Association for Justice, and a practicing maritime attorney. Their comments on the proposed policy are summarized in table 3. MARAD is reviewing the comments, and officials said that it will promulgate a final policy as soon as practicable.

---

[22]78 Fed. Reg. 30,956 (May 23, 2013).

Table 3: Differing Viewpoints on the Cruise Vessel Security and Safety Act (CVSSA) Training Certification Provision

Maritime Administration (MARAD) training certification

CVSSA language: The Administrator of the Maritime Administration may certify organizations in the United States and abroad that offer the curriculum for training and certification [for crime prevention, detection, evidence preservation and reporting].[a]

Cruise Lines International Association (CLIA)	CLIA had both questions and suggested changes for MARAD to consider when developing its final policy. Specifically, CLIA addressed the process MARAD plans to use to certify training providers that may have already been independently certified, and requested that MARAD provide additional details on the qualifications it will be looking for in a training provider in order to obtain certification, among other items. CLIA also made numerous suggestions including a request for a quicker turnaround for certification approval and for MARAD not to publicize the course materials of certified training providers for proprietary reasons, among other items.
Cruise victim advocacy group's perspective	International Cruise Victims' (ICV) comments included a request to make the certification mandatory, as well as for MARAD to have responsibility for issuing uniform course completion certificates to training providers. ICV also asked about the criteria MARAD plans to use to evaluate training providers. Additionally, ICV sought more clarity from MARAD on the frequency of the compliance audits that MARAD plans to perform for training providers, among other items.
Other interested parties' perspectives:	Two others commented on MARAD's proposed policy. These included the American Association for Justice (AAJ) as well as a maritime attorney. First, AAJ commented that the certification program does not provide immunity to cruise lines for failure to preserve evidence; instead it is simply a certification of a training standard and nothing more. Second, AAJ urged caution in relying on the certification program to successfully and skillfully preserve evidence, as those that are certified remain cruise line personnel and are not agents of the government. The maritime lawyer had one main concern about the transparency of the training provider, and would like to see MARAD require cruise lines to post on their websites their training providers and the names of the crew who are certified.

Source: Notice of proposed new policy comments provided to MARAD.

[a]46 U.S.C. § 3508(a).

The FBI and the Coast Guard Have Fully Implemented CVSSA Crime Data Reporting Requirements

The FBI and the Coast Guard have fully implemented the CVSSA provisions regarding crime data reporting. Specifically, the FBI is responsible for implementing two main areas of the CVSSA: reviewing safety guides that the cruise lines prepare[23] and reporting CVSSA crime data (regarding crimes that occur onboard cruise ships) to the Coast Guard which publishes it on a public website.[24] FBI officials reported that they provide data for cases no longer under investigation, as stated in the CVSSA. The CVSSA identifies eight crimes that, if within the FBI's jurisdiction, cruise lines must report to the FBI.[25] These crimes are homicide, suspicious death, missing U.S. national, kidnapping, assault with serious bodily injury, firing or tampering with the vessel, theft of money or property in excess of $10,000, and certain sexual assault offenses.[26] The CVSSA then requires the Coast Guard to publish on its website a statistical compilation of all allegations of CVSSA crimes reported to the FBI that are no longer under FBI investigation.[27] The data are to be updated at least quarterly, aggregated by cruise line, and each

---

[23]46 U.S.C. § 3507(c)(1). FBI officials told us that after the CVSSA was enacted, the cruise lines sent them their safety guides for the FBI to review, and the FBI provided comments back to the cruise lines, as required.

[24] Id. at § 3507(g)(4). While both the Coast Guard and the FBI have implementation responsbilities for the crime-reporting requirements in the CVSSA, the vast majority of the work in implementing the crime reporting provision of the CVSSA falls to the FBI. The Coast Guard's role is ensuring that the crime statistics that the FBI provides to it are posted on the Coast Guard's website in a timely manner, and it has done so. The website where the crime statistics are posted is *http://www.uscg.mil/hq/cg2/cgis/CruiseLine.asp.*

[25]46 U.S.C. § 3507(g)(3)(A). The FBI has jurisdiction to investigate an alleged crime if (1) the vessel, regardless of registry, is owned, in whole or in part, by a United States person, regardless of the nationality of the victim or perpetrator, and the incident occurs when the vessel is within the admiralty and maritime jurisdiction of the United States and outside the jurisdiction of any state; (2) the incident concerns an offense by or against a United States national committed outside the jurisdiction of any nation; (3) the incident occurs in the Territorial Sea of the United States, regardless of the nationality of the vessel, the victim, or the perpetrator; or (4) the incident concerns a victim or perpetrator who is a United States national on a vessel during a voyage that departed from or will arrive at a U.S. port. 46 U.S.C. § 3507(g)(3)(B).

[26]The sexual assault offenses are aggravated sexual abuse, sexual abuse, sexual abuse of a minor, and abusive sexual contact. Prior to the CVSSA, in March 2007, the FBI, the Coast Guard, and CLIA reached an agreement on voluntary, standardized protocols for CLIA member lines to report allegations of serious violations of U.S. law committed aboard cruise vessels. The agreement listed eight categories of incidents that are to be reported by CLIA members to the nearest FBI field office or legal attaché office. These incidents are identical to those listed in the CVSSA.

[27]46 U.S.C. § 3507(g)(4).

type of crime is to be identified including whether it was committed by a passenger or a crew member. Figure 2 explains the FBI's general process for receiving a CVSSA-related crime report and, if appropriate, opening and closing its investigation of a CVSSA-related crime.

Figure 2: Law Enforcement Process for Investigation of Cruise Crime within FBI's Jurisdiction

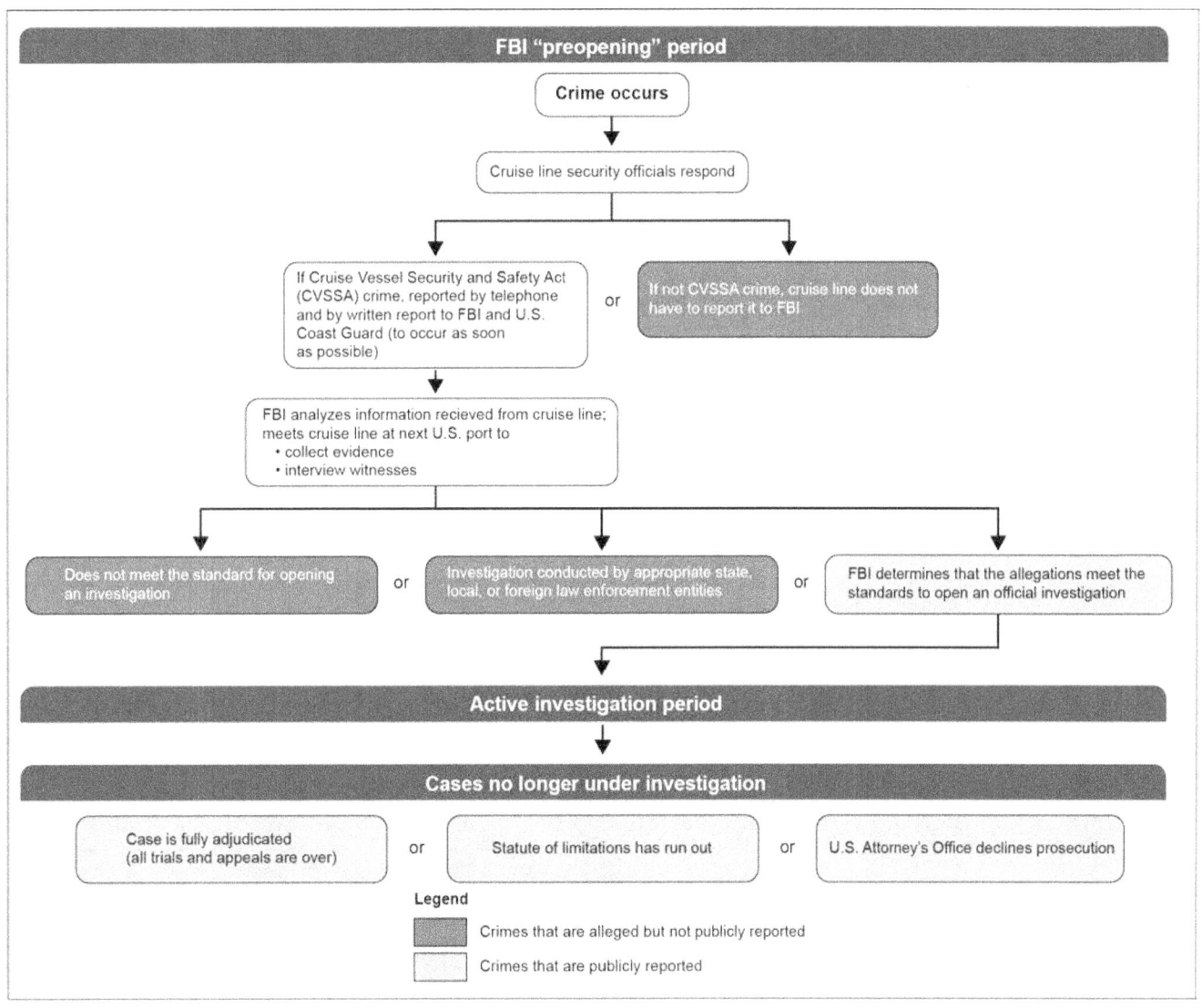

Source: GAO analysis of FBI interviews

Note: Figure 2 describes the general process law enforcement might use to investigate a cruise vessel crime. However, each case is different and the facts and circumstances will drive how the case is approached. Additionally, the FBI continues to gather information and evidence during the "active investigation period." However, we did not include specific methods the FBI uses because the purpose of this graphic is to show which alleged crimes are eventually reported publicly, and not to detail the FBI's investigative methods.

FBI Involvement—"Pre-opening" Period

When an alleged crime occurs aboard a cruise vessel, according to cruise line officials, the security officer onboard the vessel typically receives notification of the alleged crime. If the alleged crime is believed to be a CVSSA-related crime, the security officer is usually required to notify the vessel owner, since under the CVSSA it is the owner's responsibility to report any CVSSA crime to the FBI and the Coast Guard as soon as possible.[28] FBI officials stated that initial reports of crimes can come in varying forms, but generally for CVSSA crimes, they are notified within 24 hours by telephone. FBI officials also stated that, in most instances, they are relying on cruise vessel personnel to preserve the crime scene aboard the vessel since the FBI cannot typically get to a cruise vessel until it arrives in a United States port.[29] To help address these circumstances, the FBI has provided the cruise lines with a standard form for detailing initial information about the alleged crime that includes a description of the incident; the names of victims, witnesses, and suspects; any statements made by those involved; and any evidence preserved (rape kits, video recordings, photos, etc.). The cruise lines are to send this form to the FBI and Coast Guard as soon as possible after the crime is reported. The FBI considers the information as it determines what further actions need to be taken.

According to a cruise victim advocate group's official, this "pre-opening" phase has been a stated source of concern for the group because of the following issues:

- **Law enforcement response:** At sea, unlike on land, generally, a crime victim cannot call 911 to reach an independent local law enforcement authority. Instead, it is the responsibility of the cruise line's security personnel to respond. This can be disconcerting to the

---

[28] 46 U.S.C. § 3507(g)(3)(A). The CVSSA also gives the cruise lines discretion to report any serious incident that does not meet the reporting requirements of the law if they wish. Officials from one cruise line we spoke with said it generally reports all crimes that occur onboard, including minor offenses, to the FBI.

[29] If the next port is a U.S. port, the FBI is to meet the vessel upon arrival. If the next port is a foreign port, the FBI works with the local foreign authorities to decide who has jurisdiction over the case. If it is determined that a foreign country has jurisdiction, it would be less likely the FBI would also open its own investigation, according to the FBI.

victim of a crime, particularly if the alleged perpetrator is a cruise line employee. An ICV official stated that the group realizes that it is the cruise line's responsibility to respond initially, but the ICV believes that victims should be given immediate access to a private phone and contact information to call the FBI directly, and other support organizations.[30]

- **Jurisdiction:** Cruise vessels generally sail through multiple local and foreign jurisdictions during a cruise. A cruise victim advocate group official stated that this can result in a victim feeling confused in dealing with the different legal systems.[31] Depending on where the reported crime occurs, there can be several foreign ports that the cruise line may visit before arriving back in the United States. Each of these foreign jurisdictions may investigate the crime if it so chooses.

- **Evidence integrity:** Cruise vessel personnel preserve crime scene evidence until law enforcement personnel board the vessel to begin reviewing the allegations, generally upon the vessel arriving at a U.S. port. For cruise victim advocates, this raises questions about evidence preservation, conflict of interest, the feasibility of conducting an investigation days after a crime may have occurred, and the potential contamination of a crime scene if other jurisdictions investigate prior to the vessel arriving back in the United States.

In response to these concerns, FBI officials stated that they believe it is important to have cruise line security officials begin some evidence preservation work. They added that this is important given that there is no law enforcement agency onboard and that the FBI interviews and evidence collection are generally conducted when the cruise vessel has arrived in a U.S. port. To help support this effort, the FBI has provided

---

[30]The CVSSA does require cruise lines to provide victims of alleged sexual assault with free and immediate access to contact information for law enforcement, hotline services, and others and a private telephone line and Internet connection by which the individual may confidentially access law enforcement, an attorney, and information and support services. 46 U.S.C. § 3507(d)(5).

[31]If a crime occurs outside the United States' jurisdiction, State Department officials said that if they are notified of a cruise vessel crime involving a U.S. citizen, the local embassy or consulate will provide assistance to that U.S. citizen, if needed, and coordinate with the FBI.

CLIA with information on how to preserve crime scenes.[32] FBI officials in all field offices we visited told us they have never been concerned about the information they received or the integrity of an investigation as a result of the security officer being a cruise line employee. Most cruise line officials mentioned that the circumstances of an international cruise—where no independent law enforcement agency is available in international waters—may make it necessary for their security personnel to begin preserving evidence and collecting information while the vessel is still at sea to assist law enforcement personnel. FBI officials in one port city noted that they had seen an improvement in evidence preservation since the CVSSA came into law.

FBI Investigation—Active Investigation Period

Upon boarding the vessel, the FBI can more readily gather evidence, interview witnesses, and survey the crime scene. If the alleged crime meets the standard for opening an investigation, the FBI will open an investigation and certain statistics about the case are to be published on the Coast Guard's website when the case is closed. Whether the FBI opens an investigation depends on a number of factors related to the facts and circumstances of each case. However, for a crime allegation to eventually appear on the Coast Guard's public website, under the law, an investigation would have to have been officially opened by the FBI.

FBI Investigation—Cases No Longer under Investigation, or "Closed" Cases

According to FBI officials, an open case may no longer be under investigation if (1) the case has reached a final disposition in court (e.g., a verdict was rendered and appeals have concluded); (2) the statute of limitations has run out; and (3) at some point following the opening of an official investigation, the U.S. Attorney declines prosecution. Once a case is closed, FBI provides statistics on these closed cases to the Coast Guard for posting on the website.

However, there is a difference between the number of reported cases and the number of closed cases. Table 4 identifies alleged CVSSA crimes reported to the FBI by year, and table 5 identifies closed CVSSA cases published on the Coast Guard's public website by year. As tables 4 and 5 demonstrate, there were 287 alleged CVSSA crimes reported to the FBI

---

[32]However, in the information provided to CLIA, the FBI cautions that cruise line personnel should not be "collecting evidence" nor does their effort to preserve a crime scene create an agency relationship such that cruise vessel or other maritime vessel personnel are deemed to be acting as agents of the government, or vice versa.

during this nearly 4-year time period and 81 CVSSA crimes that were published on the website as closed.

Table 4: Alleged CVSSA Crimes Reported to the FBI by Cruise Lines from January 2010 through September 2013

Crime	2010	2011	2012	2013 (January-September)	Total
Homicide	0	0	0	0	0
Death-suspicious	1	3	0	2	6
Missing U.S. national	3	5	7	7	22
Kidnapping	0	0	0	0	0
Assault with serious bodily injury	12	3	10	12	37
Firing or tampering with vessel	1	0	1	1	3
Theft greater than $10,000	19	16	15	13	63
Sexual assault	50	43	30	33	156
Total allegations	**86**	**70**	**63**	**68**	**287**

Source: GAO analysis of FBI data.

Note: According to FBI officials, the FBI receives reports of alleged serious violations of U.S. law directly from the cruise lines in accordance with the CVSSA. The FBI then assesses the reports and classifies the allegations into one of the eight serious violations outlined in the CVSSA.

Table 5: Alleged CVSSA Crimes No Longer under Investigation by the FBI (Published on Coast Guard Website) from January 2010 through September 2013

Crime	2010	2011	2012	2013 (January-September)	Total
Homicide	0	0	0	0	0
Death-suspicious	4	0	1	0	5
Missing U.S. national	0	0	0	1	1
Kidnapping	0	0	0	0	0
Assault with serious bodily injury	3	3	0	2	8
Firing or tampering with vessel	0	0	1	0	1
Theft greater than $10,000	0	0	2	0	2
Sexual assault	28	13	11	12	64
Total crimes no longer under investigation	**35**	**16**	**15**	**15**	**81**

Source: GAO analysis of Coast Guard data.

While the FBI reporting of CVSSA crime data is consistent with the law, these data have some limitations. For example, the crime data currently reported are limited in that (1) allegations for which investigations are not opened are not reported, (2) the data reported are not timely, and (3) the data reported are not put into context that would provide the public with the magnitude of crime on vessels, as discussed below.

- **Allegations for which investigations are not opened are never published:** As shown in tables 4 and 5, there are more than three times the number of alleged crimes reported to the FBI by the cruise lines than the CVSSA requires the FBI to post publicly. The data in table 4 on alleged crimes are not available publicly. According to a cruise victim advocate we interviewed, and to some members of Congress, there are questions about whether the public is adequately informed about the numbers of alleged CVSSA crimes on cruise lines. An official from a cruise victim advocacy group we interviewed stated that without complete data on the crimes that have occurred on cruise vessels, the public may not have the necessary information to make informed decisions about cruise travel. However, information on allegations of crime also may not accurately reflect crime on cruise vessels, as some allegations may be unfounded.

- **Data reported are not timely:** There can be a lag between the time an alleged crime is reported to the FBI and the time a case is closed. According to an FBI official, the crime data that are posted on Coast Guard's website represent incidents that may have occurred months or years in the past. Depending on the progression of a case, this may be due to the length of the investigation, criminal trial, or any appeals. As a result, crimes published on the public website often do not align with the quarter, and sometimes the year, in which the crime occurred. An official from a cruise victim advocacy group we interviewed commented that the significant time lapse from when a crime allegedly occurs to when it is ultimately reported on the public website results in the public getting less valuable information about crimes that may have occurred onboard cruise vessels.

- **Data reported without any context for comparison:** According to a CLIA official, appropriate context is needed when presenting the CVSSA crime data figures so that the public can determine how cruise vessel crime rates compare with land-based crime rates. The FBI's Uniform Crime Reports (UCR) collects crime statistics from over

18,000 city, university and college, county, state and tribal, and federal law enforcement agencies.[33] In an effort to provide more detail on the comparative prevalence of cruise crimes, one cruise line and CLIA have included data that compare cruise line crime rates for homicide, rape, and assault with serious bodily injury with similar land-based crime rate statistics from the UCR for homicide, forcible rape, and aggravated assault.[34] As we discuss below, while the UCR comparison has some limitations, CLIA officials commented that providing this comparison would provide potential cruise passengers with more transparent and comprehensive crime statistics. In addition to using rates to compare the prevalence of cruise vessel crime with the prevalence of land-based crime, presenting cruise crime data in a rate-based format may also be useful in comparing crime statistics among cruise lines.

In July 2013, CLIA officials stated that certain cruise lines would begin reporting additional crime data on their websites. According to CLIA, in August 2013, six cruise lines—which account for over 90 percent of the North American cruise passengers—began to voluntarily report on their respective websites the number of alleged CVSSA crimes that had been reported onboard their cruise vessels.[35] Officials from one of these cruise lines stated that they were volunteering to report this information to be more transparent about alleged crimes reported on their vessels. The data presented on their respective websites provide more information than they are required to report to the FBI—as the cruise line website information includes all alleged CVSSA crimes that have been reported regardless of FBI jurisdiction, even if the allegation of a crime is later determined to be unfounded.

---

[33]The UCR was conceived in 1929 by the International Association of Chiefs of Police to meet the need for reliable uniform crime statistics for the nation. In 1930, the FBI was tasked with collecting, publishing, and archiving those statistics. The FBI produces three annual publications: *Crime in the United States, Law Enforcement Officers Killed and Assaulted,* and *Hate Crime Statistics.* The crime data are submitted either through a state UCR program or directly to the FBI's UCR Program.

[34] Although the crime data on CLIA's website are presented through the end of 2012, the UCR's definition of forcible rape was updated in January 2013 to be more broad and include rape of a male or a female. CLIA indicated that it would require its members to update their definitions as the UCR definitions change.

[35]CLIA reports a subset of these data on its website as well. One of the six cruise lines is a corporation that reported the crime data in aggregate for its four North American–based cruise line subsidiaries.

However, methodological factors may limit the usefulness of these data for consumers. For example, there are some limitations associated with the UCR data comparisons that one cruise line and CLIA are making, in that, only certain CVSSA crimes—violent crimes—can be reasonably compared with the UCR crimes because of definitional differences and the lack of comparison crimes identified in the UCR. In addition, some factors that explain the relatively low rate of alleged cruise vessel crimes compared with UCR land-based crime rates include the fact that passengers are in a confined cruise vessel environment where all persons and items brought onboard are screened, camera surveillance is ubiquitous, security personnel are present, and the demographic profile of the passengers on cruise vessels does not necessarily compare well with the profile of a major U.S. city (average income, for example). As a result, the differences presented by these two environments make the comparison between a cruise vessel environment and a land-based community challenging. A CLIA official commented that despite these limitations, the UCR is still viewed as the only national data set of reported crimes that can be used to make crime comparisons. According to a criminal justice researcher familiar with the cruise industry data, the UCR is being used as a comparison baseline in part because of the lack of an alternative baseline for comparing crime data, and while there may be some limitations, the comparative analysis is appropriate.[36] While the presentation of the data on the cruise lines' and CLIA's websites may have limitations, the methodology for comparison generally appears sound and this voluntary crime data reporting is more comprehensive than what CVSSA currently requires.

In July 2013, legislation was introduced in the Senate and House that would amend the CVSSA, including the FBI's crime-reporting requirements, among other provisions.[37] These bills propose amending the CVSSA so that a statistical compilation of all alleged crimes, including non-CVSSA crimes, reported by cruise lines to the FBI, irrespective of

---

[36]There is precedent for the collection of alleged crime information across institutions for comparison purposes. For example, the Jeanne Clery Disclosure of Campus Security Policy and Campus Crime Statistics Act requires colleges and universities participating in federal financial aid programs to maintain and disclose statistics on certain alleged crimes. 20 U.S.C. § 1092(f). According to the Department of Education, the goal of this regulation is to provide students, and their families, as higher education consumers, with accurate, complete, and timely information about safety so they can make informed decisions.

[37]S.1340, 113th Cong. (2013); H.R. 2800,113th Cong. (2013).

their investigative status, would be publicly posted, quarterly, on a new website maintained by the Department of Transportation. Under the proposed legislation, the allegation data would identify whether each crime was committed (or allegedly committed) by a passenger or crew member and whether it was against a minor. The bills also propose that cruise lines report CVSSA-type crimes within the FBI's jurisdiction to the FBI and the nearest U.S. consulate within 4 hours of the crime occurring, among other items.[38] In July 2013, these bills were referred to the Senate Committee on Commerce, Science and Transportation and the House Committee on Transportation and Infrastructure's Subcommittee on Coast Guard and Maritime Transportation, respectively.

The efforts of both the cruise lines and Congress could improve the completeness, timeliness, and context for crime data on cruise vessels. However, as previously stated, the cruise lines are publishing their information voluntarily, and it is unknown if they will continue to do so. Also, there are some consistency issues in how the data are reported, with one cruise company reporting its data in aggregate—combining the crime data of all of its North American subsidiary cruise lines into a single data set for reporting—while other cruise companies report crime data by individual company or by subsidiary cruise line. In addition, the cruise lines currently do not report crime in a rate-based format, which would allow for easier comparison among cruise lines. If enacted into the law, the proposed amendments to the CVSSA, introduced in July 2013, could also improve the timeliness, relevance, and transparency of cruise vessel crime data available to the public. As of November 2013, however, the cruise lines' voluntary reporting had just begun and the CVSSA bills remained in committee, and thus we cannot assess whether, or to what extent, these efforts may address the data limitations.

---

[38]Currently, CVSSA requires an alleged crime to be reported to the FBI "as soon as possible," and it does not require the nearest U.S. consulate to be notified. 46 U.S.C. 3507(g)(3)(A).

The Cruise Industry Made Changes after the Costa Concordia Accident and Potential International Regulations Remain under Consideration

The cruise industry responded to the *Costa Concordia* accident by reviewing safety practices and implementing changes across the industry and potential international regulatory actions are under consideration at the IMO. The Coast Guard began witnessing passenger musters in February 2012, soon after the *Costa Concordia* accident, and has participated in a mass rescue exercise involving a cruise vessel.[39]

The Cruise Industry Adopted Safety-Related Policies Identified following the *Costa Concordia* Accident

In response to the *Costa Concordia* accident, CLIA initiated an operational safety review and member cruise lines adopted 10 safety-related policies.[40] According to CLIA's Operational Safety Review Executive Summary, the review was guided by cruise industry members with the advice and input of an independent panel of safety experts.[41] Suggested policies were discussed and developed within CLIA's Operational Safety Review's Task Force, made up of senior industry executives from CLIA's member lines with responsibility for maritime safety, and approved by the chief executive officers (CEO) of member lines. The resulting 10 policies relate to various safety enhancements, such as improvements to passenger musters, vessel passage planning, and life jacket stowage. CLIA announced these policies throughout 2012, as shown in figure 3.

---

[39]Musters are mandatory exercises conducted on cruise vessels to ensure passengers are informed of safety protocols while onboard the vessel, including emergency evacuation procedures.

[40]CLIA announced its Operational Safety Review on January 27, 2012, about 2 weeks after the *Costa Concordia* accident. CLIA officials said they completed their review in December 2012.

[41]CLIA, *Operational Safety Review Executive Summary*, accessed June 14, 2013, http://www.cruising.org/regulatory/cruise-industry-policies/cruise-industry-operational-safety-review. The panel of experts included a former chairman of the U.S. NTSB; a former rear admiral in the Royal Navy and head of the United Kingdom's Marine Accident Investigation Branch; a former director, Office of Marine Safety, U.S. NTSB; and a former head and executive director of the European Maritime Safety Agency.

Figure 3: Timeline of CLIA Actions Relative to the Costa Concordia Accident

Costa Concordia accident
January 13, 2012

CLIA announces operational safety review
January 27, 2012

Italy makes Costa Concordia safety technical investigation available to the International Maritime Organization (IMO)
May 14, 2013

CLIA announces policies

(4)						(10)						
(3)		(6)				(9)						
(1)	(2)	(5)		(7)		(8)						

Jan. Feb. Mar. Apr. May Jun. Jul. Aug. Sept. Oct. Nov. Dec. | Jan. Feb. Mar. Apr. May Jun.
2012 | 2013

Cruise Lines International Association (CLIA) policies and date announced since Costa Condordia accident

Date announced		Policy	Brief description
February 9, 2012	(1)	Passenger muster	Embarking passengers are to muster prior to departure from port.
April 24, 2012	(2)	Passage planning	Makes IMO and industry bridge team management standards mandatory for cruise vessels; specifies certain passage plan briefing requirements and encourages bridge team members to raise operational concerns without fear of retribution.
	(3)	Bridge access	To prevent distractions and disruptions, access to the bridge is to be limited to persons having operationally related functions during certain defined periods, such as when the vessel is arriving at and departing from port.
	(4)	Excess life jackets	Additional life jackets are to be stored in public spaces readily accessible in an emergency.
June 26, 2012	(5)	Recording nationality of passengers	Along with names and other relevant details, the nationality of passengers is to be recorded, kept ashore, and be made readily available to search and rescue services.
	(6)	Common elements of musters and emergency instructions	Twelve common elements are to be communicated to passengers in musters and emergency instructions.
September 20, 2012	(7)	Lifeboat loading for training purposes	Every 6 months, one or more lifeboats are operated in the water while filled to capacity with crew members wearing life jackets to facilitate training of lifeboat and embarkation/boarding station crew.
November 15, 2012	(8)	Harmonizing of bridge procedures	Bridge procedures are to be harmonized within companies.
	(9)	Securing heavy objects	Heavy objects are to be secured (restricted from movement so as not to cause injury) either permanently, when not in use, or during severe weather, as appropriate.
	(10)	Location of life jacket stowage	Life jackets equal to or greater than the number required are to be stowed in proximity to either muster stations or lifeboat embarkation points on newly constructed vessels.

Source: GAO analysis of CLIA policies.

As a condition of CLIA membership, CEOs of all member cruise lines had to attest in writing that their companies had adopted the 10 policies and had included them in their companies' safety management systems (SMS), according to CLIA officials.[42] These officials said they expected cruise lines to implement most of the policies upon the dates of their announcement.[43] Officials noted that they received written attestations from member cruise line CEOs at different times following the announcements; however, all had provided them as of July 2013. As a matter of international regulation, once a policy has been included in a company's SMS, the policy is subject to routine external audits. These audits are conducted by vessels' flag states (or classification societies acting on their behalf), which are responsible for ensuring that a vessel's SMS is in compliance with the ISM Code and that the company operates the vessel in accordance with the SMS, among other things.[44] Almost all cruise vessels visiting U.S. ports are registered (flagged) in other countries, and are therefore subject to SMS compliance audits by their flag states. When foreign-flagged cruise vessels visit U.S. ports, their SMSs are also subject to verification by the Coast Guard in its role as a port state control authority.[45] Coast Guard officials said their port state control boarding officers review the validity of the certificates issued by a vessel's flag state and also perform spot checks of a vessel's compliance with its SMS, and noted that their review of a vessel's SMS is less in-depth than a flag state's review. Officials also explained that the Coast Guard may check items in a vessel's SMS that go beyond domestic or

---

[42]An SMS is a structured and documented system enabling company personnel to implement effectively the company safety and environmental protection policy.

[43]One policy—the location of life jacket stowage policy—went into effect on July 1, 2013, for newly constructed cruise vessels. CLIA officials said that they did not expect cruise lines to implement the harmonization of bridge procedures policy and the securing heavy objects policy upon the dates of their announcement (November 15, 2012).

[44]As part of enforcing the ISM Code, flag states (or organizations recognized by the flag administrations, such as classification societies) audit company and vessel compliance with its SMS, and issue documents of compliance and safety management certificates that are valid for 5 years, subject to periodic verification. The ISM Code also requires that companies perform annual internal safety audits to ensure compliance with their SMSs.

[45]As previously discussed, through its Port State Control Program, the Coast Guard routinely boards foreign-flagged vessels operating in U.S. waters to verify that they are in compliance with applicable international conventions and U.S. laws and regulations. When the Coast Guard identifies vessels that are not in substantial compliance with applicable laws or regulations, it is responsible for imposing controls to ensure the vessels are brought into compliance.

international regulations—such as the 10 CLIA policies shown in figure 3—but said that any deficiencies found would merely be subject to correction rather than vessel detention because such items are self imposed rather than part of any regulation. However, Coast Guard officials noted that a series of such deficiencies might indicate a lack of implementation of the SMS which could result in more serious actions by Coast Guard.

To facilitate CLIA's operational safety review following the *Costa Concordia* accident, each member cruise line was to conduct a review of its own safety practices and procedures and collaborate to share best practices. The reviews conducted by the five cruise lines we interviewed varied in scope and outcomes. For example, according to a document provided by one company, it conducted a safety review that examined nine areas of its cruise operations—such as emergency management and damage control—and officials said this review resulted in over 500 recommendations. Another cruise line provided documentation showing that its review, conducted by an outside entity, focused on six objectives that in many cases relate to the human aspect of safety and emergency response—such as leadership involvement, teamwork and training, and safety culture—and the review resulted in 26 observations for further consideration. Representatives of the five cruise lines we spoke with identified some examples of changes they have made, or are making, after reviewing their safety procedures following the *Costa Concordia* accident. They include the following:

- One cruise line, as part of its quality assurance processes, reported that it has its most qualified captains visit vessels and observe staff to determine whether they are fostering an open atmosphere on the bridge. These captains are to ensure that senior bridge officers are making their thoughts and intentions known, and that junior bridge officers challenge senior officers if they are unclear about orders or have concerns. This emphasis on bridge team management aligns with the new CLIA "Passage Planning" policy where, among other things, bridge team members are encouraged to raise operational concerns without fear of retribution.

- Another cruise line reported that it changed the duty of managing the vessel mustering process from the captain of the vessel to the hotel director, to alleviate extra burden on the captain during an emergency. It also changed its mustering policy, so if a passenger refuses to muster prior to departure, then that passenger is not allowed to travel.

- Another cruise line reported that it sent its officers to receive testing to assess how they will react during the stress of an emergency; the suitability of their leadership style; and human factors such as approachability, reliability, and acceptance of change. CLIA officials also said testing of crew to assess how they will react during the stress of an emergency was a topic of in-depth discussion during its operational safety review following the *Costa Concordia* accident.

Representatives from all five cruise lines we spoke with said they have included, or plan to include, the safety-related changes they have made as a result of their internal reviews into their SMSs.

International Safety Measures Are Under Consideration and the Coast Guard Has Taken Some Initial Actions

IMO Adopted Muster Regulation and Is Considering Other Potential Measures

IMO's Maritime Safety Committee (MSC)—a key IMO committee charged with addressing all matters related to the safety of shipping—has adopted one regulation, issued 18 interim safety recommendations, and is considering additional safety-related measures that it may take following the *Costa Concordia* accident. Specifically, MSC adopted a regulation in June 2013 to be effective on January 1, 2015, which requires that newly embarked passengers muster prior to or immediately upon departure, instead of within 24 hours, as stated in current regulations.[46] According to a Coast Guard official, in the case of the *Costa Concordia* accident, the passengers that had embarked at the previous port had not yet participated in a muster drill before the accident occurred.[47]

---

[46]In June 2013, the IMO Marine Safety Committee adopted amendments to the SOLAS convention, regulations III/19.2.2 and III/19.2.3.

[47]According to the Italian government report on the safety technical investigation for the *Costa Concordia* accident, 1,270 of the 3,206 passengers had participated in a muster drill, while the remaining passengers received safety instructions by video.

IMO's MSC has also issued 18 interim safety recommendations for passenger vessel companies to implement on a voluntary basis.[48] Many of these recommendations closely align with the 10 CLIA policies discussed above. For example, as with CLIA's policy, IMO recommends that companies record the nationality of persons onboard for purposes of coordination during emergencies.[49] However, in some cases the IMO recommendations offer additional guidance. For example, in addition to recommending that passenger vessels carry additional life jackets in public spaces (similar to CLIA's policy), IMO recommends that companies consider providing life jackets that are similarly designed and can be donned in a similar manner to avoid confusion. Following the release of the *Costa Concordia* safety technical accident investigation report in May 2013, the MSC working group responsible for developing these 18 interim recommendations expressed the view that, in the future, a decision will need to be made on their final status.

Following the *Costa Concordia* accident, the MSC created a long-term action plan to facilitate the consideration of measures resulting from the accident. According to a MSC report, MSC uses the action plan to document proposals from IMO member governments and international organizations. The action plan is not publicly available; however, a Coast Guard official present at the June 2013 MSC meeting said the plan contains about 20 items and can be viewed as a list of issues—similar to the list of 18 interim safety recommendations—on which the MSC may

[48]In June 2012, IMO's MSC issued a circular with 5 interim recommendations, and has subsequently updated the circular twice, for a total of 18 interim recommendations. These 18 recommendations address life jackets onboard passenger vessels, emergency instructions for passengers, common elements of musters and emergency instructions, passenger muster policy, access of personnel to the navigating bridge and avoiding distractions, harmonization of bridge navigational procedures, voyage planning, recording the nationality of persons on board, lifeboat loading for training purposes, securing heavy objects, and inclinometer (rolling motion) data for the voyage data recorder. More complete information can be accessed by creating a public account on *http://webaccounts.imo.org,* and searching for the circular that lists the 18 interim recommendations (MSC.1/Circ.1446/Rev.2).

[49]Department of State officials said they had a difficult time determining who the U.S. citizens were that were onboard the *Costa Concordia* at the time of the accident. Officials said the vessel's manifest contained only last names and first initials of passengers and did not have citizenship information, making it difficult for them to determine who the U.S citizens were so they could render assistance.

take further action.[50] This action could include a variety of outcomes, including the development of international regulations. Figure 4 summarizes the main actions of IMO following the *Costa Concordia* accident.

---

[50]This same Coast Guard official noted that the long-term action plan was not intended to include only issues that can be linked directly to the *Costa Concordia* accident. He said the plan also includes issues that were already under consideration by MSC when the accident occurred. At the most recent MSC meeting (June 2013), MSC instructed the IMO Secretariat to revise the long-term action plan with a view to clearly identify whether proposed actions are related to existing issues or are new issues arising from the loss of the *Costa Concordia*. The Coast Guard informed us that this revision has been completed, but noted that the action plan has not been finalized and therefore continues to not be publicly available.

Figure 4: Timeline of IMO MSC Actions following the Costa Concordia Accident

Costa Concordia accident
January 13, 2012

Italy makes Costa Concordia safety technical investigation available to the International Maritime Organization (IMO)
May 14, 2013

Jan. 2012 | Feb. | Mar. | Apr. | May | Jun. | Jul. | Aug. | Sept. | Oct. | Nov. | Dec. | Jan. 2013 | Feb. | Mar. | Apr. | May | Jun. | Jul.

90th session of the IMO Maritime Safety Committee, May 16-25, 2012

Established working group to consider potential actions IMO may take as a result of the Costa Concordia accident.

Issued circular recommending 5 interim measures to enhance passenger vessel safety.

Adopted a resolution inviting IMO member governments to recommend that passenger vessel companies conduct a voluntary review of operational safety measures.

Developed a long-term action plan on passenger vessel safety that incorporates proposals submitted by member states and international organizations.

91st session of the IMO Maritime Safety Committee, November 26-30, 2012

Revised circular recommending interim measures to enhance passenger vessel safety (added 4 new interim measures, for a total of 9).

Revised long-term action plan on passenger vessel safety, based on progress made at the 91st Maritime Safety Committee session.

92nd session of the IMO Maritime Safety Committee, June 12-21, 2013

Adopted amendments to international regulation to require musters of newly embarked passengers prior to or immediately upon departure.

Revised circular recommending interim measures to enhance passenger vessel safety (added 9 new interim measures, for a total of 18).

Invited Italy to provide more technical information on the Costa Concordia safety technical investigation report and invited member governments and international organizations to submit detailed comments and proposals related to the Italian report at the next Maritime Safety Committee session.

Updated the revised long-term action plan.

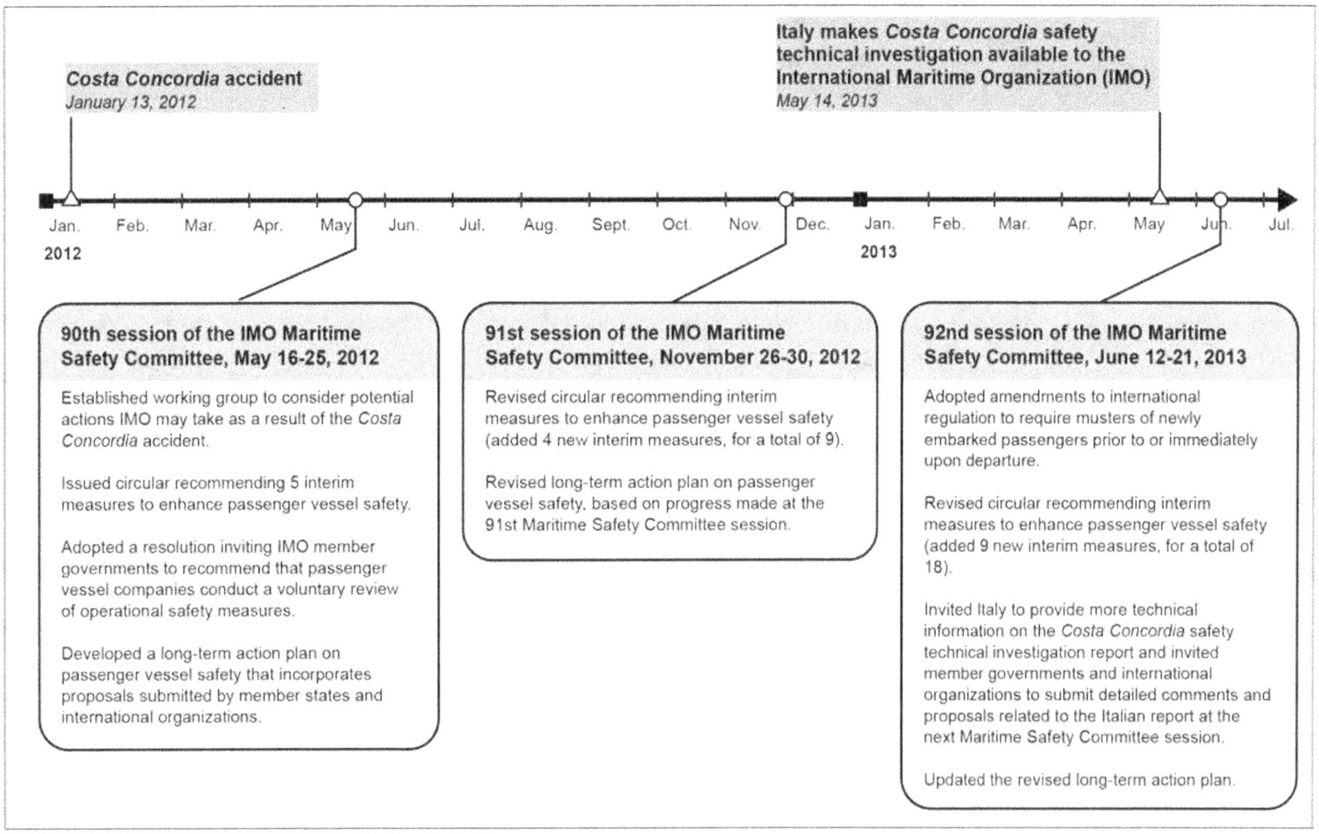

Source: GAO analysis of IMO actions

Although IMO is considering additional measures that may become regulations, it could be years before they take effect, and the Coast Guard can then enforce them through its port state control inspections.[51] In the interim, the one new regulation, adopted in June 2013, requires newly embarked passengers to muster prior to or immediately upon departure.

---

[51] The Coast Guard generally focuses its enforcement activities on U.S. and international regulations. However, as of September 2013, we identified one international regulation and no U.S. regulations that have been adopted as a result of the Costa Concordia accident.

Coast Guard Witnesses
Passenger Musters and
Coordinated Mass Rescue
Exercise

Although the new muster requirement does not go into effect until January 2015, the Coast Guard initiated the practice of witnessing passenger musters as part of its mandatory vessel examination program in February 2012, just weeks after the *Costa Concordia* accident. Coast Guard officials acknowledged that they are, in effect, regulating by policy; however, they said the industry is supportive of this effort and has developed a similar policy to perform passenger musters prior to departure. Coast Guard officials said that when witnessing passenger musters, the Coast Guard actively ensures they contain the elements required by current regulation. For example, they check to ensure that crew members are appropriately directing passengers to their muster stations and that passengers are instructed in how to wear a life jacket, among other things. The Coast Guard reported it has witnessed about 280 musters since its policy went into effect, and agency officials said they have not had any major concerns with the musters they have witnessed.[52]

The Coast Guard reported that it is also continuing to monitor developments resulting from the *Costa Concordia* accident and may make additional policy changes in the future. For example, the Coast Guard and the NTSB represented the United States as a "substantially interested state" in the Italian-led *Costa Concordia* accident investigation, consistent with international law.[53] Coast Guard and NTSB officials said they contributed to the investigation by interviewing U.S. passengers and providing comments on a draft of the report. A senior Coast Guard official noted some of the general lessons that all parties with an interest in the investigation have learned. For example, the official said that muster drills should be held prior to departure, vessel route changes should not be made as unilateral decisions by the captain, better control of a vessel's environment can help alleviate human error, proper training of crew to handle emergency situations is essential, and extra life jackets should be

---

[52]Coast Guard officials said they do not separately track the number of musters they have witnessed. However, the Coast Guard conducted 301 cruise vessel examinations from the beginning of the muster policy (February 2, 2012) through July 1, 2013. Officials estimated that they witnessed musters at about 280 of these examinations, and did not witness musters at the roughly 20 examinations where passengers had embarked on the vessel elsewhere.

[53]See IMO Resolution MSC.255(84). The investigating state should allow substantially interested states to interview witnesses, view and examine evidence and make copies of documents, make submissions in respect of the evidence, comment on and have their views properly reflected in the final report, and be provided with the draft and final reports.

available at locations convenient to evacuating passengers. Coast Guard officials said they are also monitoring actions being taken by CLIA and IMO, and may make policy changes in the future as they continue to review the final *Costa Concordia* report and wait for the results of the vessel salvage.[54]

Additionally, the Coast Guard has also been active in exercising scenarios related to cruise vessel evacuation and rescue. In April 2013, the Coast Guard coordinated an offshore cruise vessel rescue exercise in an effort to prepare for large-scale disasters similar to the *Costa Concordia* accident.[55] Although the Coast Guard has participated in mass rescue exercises involving cruise vessels before, the Coast Guard reported that this exercise was the largest in terms of scale and complexity in the history of the international maritime community and the Coast Guard.[56] The exercise was conducted in Freeport, Bahamas, and included Coast Guard collaboration with CLIA, three cruise lines, and the National Emergency Management Agency of the Bahamas, among others. One cruise line provided a cruise vessel that was used for the abandon vessel portion of the exercise, where we observed individuals posing as passengers boarding lifeboats that were lowered to the water and driven to shore. The second cruise line led the landing site and transportation element of the exercise, and the third cruise line led the sheltering operations element of the exercise where we observed passenger services— such as providing access to embassy consular affairs services, counseling, and minor medical services— being exercised.

---

[54]As a result of the accident, the *Costa Concordia* turned on its side and rested on the ocean floor, with a significant portion of the vessel still above water. Vessel salvage refers to the process of removing the vessel wreck. The owner of the vessel plans to have the vessel removed in one piece by refloating it and having it towed away from the coast of the Island of Giglio, Italy, where the accident occurred.

[55]This operation was the first in a 5-year mass rescue exercise series known as Black Swan. Future mass rescue operations are scheduled in Hawaii in 2015, and Norfolk, Virginia, in 2017.

[56]The Coast Guard noted that all offshore mass rescue events require significant search and rescue efforts including international communications; coordination of rescue resources; local emergency management stakeholders; international health care systems to support medical surge capacities to care for large numbers of injured personnel; coordinated landing site management; sustained care for the rescued with clothing, food, and counseling services; and transportation travel documentation and logistics planning to return the rescued to their homes.

In addition to witnessing the above actions as part of the mass rescue exercise, we observed efforts by the Department of State and Customs and Border Protection (CBP) as they exercised their respective responsibilities for managing passengers under the cruise vessel mass rescue scenario. For example, Department of State officials established a meeting room at the Freeport Airport, where they interacted with U.S. passenger evacuees to process their required passport documentation. Additionally, because Freeport is a CBP preclearance location—where departing U.S. passengers are processed through U.S. customs and immigration prior to departure to the United States—we witnessed CBP's approach for processing the surge of evacuees at the airport.[57] The Coast Guard characterized the 2013 exercise as a success, and noted that the exercise had effectively and interactively put into effect the full spectrum of vessel-to-shore mass rescue operations and identified strengths and weaknesses in existing procedures.

Agency Comments

We provided a draft of this report to the Department of Homeland Security, the Department of Justice, the Department of Transportation, the National Transportation Safety Board, and the Department of State for review and comment. The Department of Homeland Security, Department of Justice, and Department of State provided technical comments, which we incorporated as appropriate.

As arranged with your office, unless you publicly announce its contents earlier, we plan no further distribution of this report until 30 days after its issue date. At that time we will send copies of this report to the Secretary of Homeland Security, the Attorney General, the Secretary of Transportation, the Chairman of the National Transportation Safety Board, the Secretary of State, appropriate congressional committees, and other interested parties. This report will also be available at no charge on the GAO website at http://www.gao.gov.

[57]Preclearance operations are part of CBP's Office of Field Operations, which has the responsibility of managing 329 ports of entry nationwide. These operations are established via a formal agreement between the United States and host country, which allows CBP to staff officers at host airports and facilitate the customs and immigration process for passengers prior to arrival in the United States. As of September 2013, preclearance is in effect in Aruba, Bermuda, Bahamas (two locations), Ireland (two locations) and Canada (nine locations).

If you or your staff have any questions about this report, please contact me at (202) 512-9610 or caldwells@gao.gov. Contact points for our Offices of Congressional Relations and Public Affairs may be found on the last page of this report. Key contributors to this report are listed in appendix III.

Stephen L. Caldwell, Director
Homeland Security and Justice Issues

Appendix I: Key Stakeholders with Maritime Safety and Security Activities

This appendix provides information on the international and domestic organizations that play a role in the safety and security of cruise vessels. The non-U.S. stakeholders are diverse; have wide-ranging roles and responsibilities; and include international organizations, governments of nations where cruise vessels make stops or are registered, and private organizations that help ensure the safe operation of vessels. See table 6 for a list of some of the relevant international and domestic stakeholders involved in implementation of the Cruise Vessel Security and Safety Act of 2010 (CVSSA) and cruise vessel safety and security issues.

Table 6: Stakeholders with Maritime Safety and Security Activities

Organization or agency	Maritime security or safety activities
International organizations	
International Maritime Organization (IMO) IMO is a specialized agency of the United Nations with 170 member states that is responsible for developing an international regulatory framework addressing, among other things, maritime safety and security.	• Responsble for developing and maintaining a comprehensive regulatory framework for cruise vessels. • Responsble for developing international standards for vessel security and safety.
Flag state The flag state is the country in which the vessel is registered, and a flag state's control or authority over a vessel flying its flag can generally extend anywhere in the world that the vessel operates.	• Responsble for ensuring that vessels flying its flag meet all international safety standards.
Port state The port state is the country where the port is located. Port state control is the process by which a nation exercises its authority over foreign-flagged vessels operating in waters subject to the port state's jurisdiction.	• Inspects foreign vessels in national ports to verify that the condition of the vessel and its equipment complies with the requirements of international regulations and that the vessel is manned and operated in compliance with these rules.
Classification societies Classification societies are independent organizations that verify the structural strength and integrity of essential parts of the vessel's hull and its appendages, and the reliability and function of the propulsion and steering systems, power generation, and those other features and auxiliary systems that have been built into the vessel in order to maintain essential services onboard. Additionally, they verify the functionality of safety equipment and systems during inspections and verify operational procedures through audit programs.	• Develop and apply their own rules and verify compliance with international and national statutes on behalf of flag states. • Perform periodic surveys, carried out onboard the vessel, to verify that the vessel continues to meet relevant requirements.
Cruise Lines International Association (CLIA) CLIA is a trade association composed of 26 major cruise lines and represents 98 percent of the cruise line businesses operating in the United States.	• Responsble for acting as the coordinating body and conduit of information for its members in meetings with U.S. agencies at the national level. • Serves as a nongovernmental consultative organization to IMO.

Organization or agency	Maritime security or safety activities
Federal agencies[a]	
U.S. Coast Guard	• Ensures vessels in U.S. ports comply with domestic and international maritime security and safety standards.
	• Conducts initial, annual, and periodic exams of foreign-flagged cruise vessels calling in U.S. ports. This regime allows the Coast Guard to determine that the vessel is in substantial compliance with all applicable international and domestic standards.
	• Investigates marine casualties that occur on foreign cruise vessels in the navigable waters of the United States and its territories or possessions. The Coast Guard may also represent the United States as a "substantially interested state" in certain marine casualty investigations outside of U.S. jurisdiction. Furthermore, the Coast Guard and the National Transportation Safety Board have agreed to coordinate investigative responses for certain marine casualties.
	• Primary U.S. representative to IMO for all maritime policy development.
Maritime Administration (MARAD)	• MARAD is the agency within the U.S. Department of Transportation dealing with waterborne transportation. Among other things, it promotes the viability of U.S.-registered (flagged) vessels moving in domestic and international commerce. Almost all cruise vessels servicing the United States, however, are foreign flagged.
	• Responsible for developing a training curriculum for mariner use of force against piracy, and may certify organizations that offer a curriculum for training in the prevention, detection, evidence preservation, and reporting of criminal activities in the international maritime environment.
Federal Bureau of Investigation (FBI)	• Responsible for investigating alleged serious crimes listed in the CVSSA that occur aboard cruise vessels and meet the jurisdictional requirements of the CVSSA.
	• Employs maritime liaison agents who are responsible for coordinating with other organizations that share responsibility for security at the nation's ports, and facilitate the sharing of information on threats and security measures.
	• Employs victim specialists who provide information and crisis intervention/emergency assistance to victims of violations that fall under FBI's investigative authority, whether charges are filed or not, to include referrals to counseling and other services available in the victim's home community.
National Transportation Safety Board (NTSB)	• NTSB's Office of Marine Safety investigates major marine accidents on or under the navigable waters, internal waters, or the territorial sea of the United States as well as accidents involving U.S.-flagged vessels worldwide to determine the probable cause and identify safety recommendations that will prevent similar events in the future.

Organization or agency	Maritime security or safety activities
Department of State	• Administers the Consular Information Program to inform U.S. citizens about potential threats to their health or safety abroad.
	• Provides assistance to U.S. citizens on cruise vacations in the event of a crime, medical issue, death, or loss of passport, among other things.
	• Works with foreign embassies and cruise companies in the event of a disaster to ensure U.S. citizens are accounted for and provided assistance—such as accommodations, clothing, and transportation home.
State and local governments	
Law enforcement agencies	• Conduct investigations into cruise vessel crime occurring within their maritime jurisdictions.
	• Except in those instances where the FBI has lead jurisdiction, coordinate with the FBI regarding alleged crimes and investigations, as appropriate.

Source: GAO analysis of organization and agency documents.

[a] There are numerous federal agencies that play a role with respect to cruise safety and security, including: (1) Customs and Border Protection, which is responsible for screening vessels, passengers, and cargo as well as extraditing suspects to law enforcement officials and making admissibility decisions for non-U.S. citizens involved in crimes, among other things; (2) Centers for Disease Control and Prevention, which conducts the vessel sanitation program to assist the cruise vessel industry in preventing and controlling the introduction, transmission, and spread of gastrointestinal illnesses on cruise vessels; and (3) United States Department of Agricultural Animal and Plant Health Inspection Service, which regulates garbage arriving from outside the United States. However, for the purposes of this report, we focus on the agencies listed in table 4 because they have significant responsbilities for implementing the CVSSA, addressing crime, and ensuring the structural safety of cruise vessels.

Appendix II: Provisions in the Cruise Vessel Security and Safety Act

This appendix provides summary information on the provisions of the Cruise Vessel Security and Safety Act, including time frames for implementation.

Table 7: Summary of Provisions in the Cruise Vessel Security and Safety Act (CVSSA)

Category	Provision	Implementation time frame
Rail heights	The vessel shall be equipped with rails that are located not less than 42 inches above the cabin deck.	Eighteen months after enactment of the CVSSA.
Peepholes/other means of identification	Each passenger stateroom and crew cabin shall be equipped with entry doors that include peepholes or other means of visual identification.	Eighteen months after enactment of the CVSSA.
Security latches and time-sensitive keys	Each passenger stateroom and crew cabin shall be equipped with security latches and time-sensitive key technology.	Required for any vessel constructed after July 2010.
Capturing images of passengers/detecting persons fallen overboard	The vessel shall integrate technology that can be used for capturing images of passengers or detecting passengers who have fallen overboard, to the extent that such technology is available.	Eighteen months after enactment of the CVSSA. Per Coast Guard Policy Letter 11-09, the Coast Guard is using a phased implementation plan to accommodate analysis and research and development. This provision is to be addressed by regulation or updated policy guidance.[a]
Acoustical hailing and warning devices	Vessels shall be equipped with a sufficient number of operable acoustic hailing or other such warning devices to provide communication capability around the entire vessel when operating in high-risk waters.	Eighteen months after enactment of the CVSSA. Per Coast Guard Policy Letter 11-09, the Coast Guard is using a phased implementation plan to accommodate analysis and research and development. This provision is to be addressed by regulation or updated policy guidance.
Video recording requirements	(1) The owner of the vessel shall maintain a video surveillance system to assist in documenting crimes on the vessel and in providing evidence for the prosecution of such crimes, as determined by the Secretary of Homeland Security. (2) The owner of the vessel shall provide to any law enforcement official performing official duties in the course and scope of an investigation, upon request, a copy of all records of video surveillance that the official believes may provide evidence of a crime reported to law enforcement officials.	Per Coast Guard Policy Letter 11-09, the Coast Guard is using a phased implementation plan to accommodate analysis, research, and development. This provision is to be addressed by regulation or updated policy guidance.

Safety information	The owner of the vessel shall have available for each passenger a guide that provides a description of medical and security personnel onboard with 24-hour contact instructions and describes the jurisdictional authority applicable to, and the law enforcement processes available for, CVSSA crimes that arise in the territorial waters of the United States, on the high seas, or in any country to be visited on the voyage. The owner of the vessel shall also provide passengers with U.S. embassy and consulate information for each country the vessel will visit during the course of the voyage.	Effective immediately upon enactment of the CVSSA.
Sexual assault	The owner of the vessel shall (1) maintain adequate antiretroviral medications to prevent sexually transmitted diseases (STD) after a sexual assault; (2) maintain on-vessel equipment and materials to perform a sexual assault medical evaluation; (3) make available at all times medical staff who have proper credentialing; and (4) prepare, provide to the patient, and maintain documentation of the exam findings.	Effective immediately upon enactment of the CVSSA.
Sexual assault, patient access to information and communications	The owner of the vessel shall provide patients free access to contact information for local law enforcement, FBI, Coast Guard, nearest U.S. embassy/consulate, and sexual assault hotline, as well as private phone line and Internet.	Effective immediately upon enactment of the CVSSA.
Confidentiality of sexual assault examination and support information	The master or other individual in charge of a vessel shall treat all information concerning an exam and post-assault counseling confidential.	Effective immediately upon enactment of the CVSSA.
Crew access to passenger staterooms	The owner of the vessel shall establish and implement procedures and restrictions concerning which crew members have access to passenger staterooms and periods during which they have access.	Effective immediately upon enactment of the CVSSA.
Logbook and reporting requirements	The owner of the vessel shall record in a logbook all complaints of CVSSA crimes, all complaints of theft of property in excess of $1,000, and all complaints of other crimes committed on any voyage that embarks or disembarks passengers in the United States. The owner of the vessel shall make the logbook available upon request to the FBI, any members of the Coast Guard, and any law enforcement officer performing official duties in the course and scope of an investigation. Logbook details shall include vessel operator, name of cruise line, flag state, age/gender of victim and assailant, description of alleged crime, vessel's position, time/date/method of initial report and law enforcement authority to which it was made, time/date of incident, total number of passengers and crew members, and case number. Additionally, the owner of the vessel shall contact the FBI by phone to report alleged CVSSA crimes, and shall furnish a written report to the Coast Guard Internet portal.	Effective immediately upon enactment of the CVSSA.

Availability and access of incident data via Coast Guard website	(1) The Secretary of Homeland Security shall maintain statistical compilation on the Internet of CVSSA crimes that are no longer under investigation by the FBI. Information shall be updated quarterly and aggregated by cruise line, and each crime shall be identified as to whether it was committed by a passenger or a crew member.	Effective immediately upon enactment of the CVSSA.
	(2) Each cruise line taking or discharging passengers in the United States shall include a link on its website to the website maintained by the Coast Guard described above.	
Maritime Administration (MARAD) certification of crew training on crime scene preservation	MARAD may certify organizations in the United States and abroad that offer a curriculum for training and certification.	No implementation requirement for MARAD. Final policy under development as of December 2013.
Crew training on crime scene preservation	The Secretary of Homeland Security, in consultation with the FBI and MARAD, shall develop minimum training standards and curricula to allow for the certification of passenger vessel security personnel, crew members, and law enforcement officials on the appropriate methods for prevention, detection, evidence preservation, and reporting of criminal activities in the international maritime environment. Beginning 2 years after standards are established, no vessel may enter a U.S. port unless there is at least one crew member onboard who is certified as having completed training.	Within 1 year of the enactment of the CVSSA.

Source: GAO summary of Cruise Vessel Security and Safety Act.

[a]The Coast Guard used Policy Letter 11-09 to set dates for compliance with CVSSA provisions in cases where the act did not provide specific time frames.

Appendix III: GAO Contact and Staff Acknowledgments

GAO Contact	Stephen L. Caldwell, (202) 512-9610 or caldwells@gao.gov.
Staff Acknowledgments	In addition to the contact named above, Dawn Hoff, Assistant Director; Jeff Jensen; Daniel Klabunde; and Michelle R. Su made significant contributions to this report. In addition, David Alexander, Michele Fejfar, and Stan Kostyla assisted with design and methodology; Tracey King provided legal support; Jessica Orr provided assistance in report preparation; and Eric Hauswirth developed the report's graphics.

GAO's Mission	The Government Accountability Office, the audit, evaluation, and investigative arm of Congress, exists to support Congress in meeting its constitutional responsibilities and to help improve the performance and accountability of the federal government for the American people. GAO examines the use of public funds; evaluates federal programs and policies; and provides analyses, recommendations, and other assistance to help Congress make informed oversight, policy, and funding decisions. GAO's commitment to good government is reflected in its core values of accountability, integrity, and reliability.
Obtaining Copies of GAO Reports and Testimony	The fastest and easiest way to obtain copies of GAO documents at no cost is through GAO's website (http://www.gao.gov). Each weekday afternoon, GAO posts on its website newly released reports, testimony, and correspondence. To have GAO e-mail you a list of newly posted products, go to http://www.gao.gov and select "E-mail Updates."
Order by Phone	The price of each GAO publication reflects GAO's actual cost of production and distribution and depends on the number of pages in the publication and whether the publication is printed in color or black and white. Pricing and ordering information is posted on GAO's website, http://www.gao.gov/ordering.htm. Place orders by calling (202) 512-6000, toll free (866) 801-7077, or TDD (202) 512-2537. Orders may be paid for using American Express, Discover Card, MasterCard, Visa, check, or money order. Call for additional information.
Connect with GAO	Connect with GAO on Facebook, Flickr, Twitter, and YouTube. Subscribe to our RSS Feeds or E-mail Updates. Listen to our Podcasts. Visit GAO on the web at www.gao.gov.
To Report Fraud, Waste, and Abuse in Federal Programs	Contact: Website: http://www.gao.gov/fraudnet/fraudnet.htm E-mail: fraudnet@gao.gov Automated answering system: (800) 424-5454 or (202) 512-7470
Congressional Relations	Katherine Siggerud, Managing Director, siggerudk@gao.gov, (202) 512-4400, U.S. Government Accountability Office, 441 G Street NW, Room 7125, Washington, DC 20548
Public Affairs	Chuck Young, Managing Director, youngc1@gao.gov, (202) 512-4800 U.S. Government Accountability Office, 441 G Street NW, Room 7149 Washington, DC 20548